Dictionary of the Rare,
Creative, and Beautiful
Words for Writers, Poets & Dreamers

Robin Devoe

Dictionary of the Rare, Creative, and Beautiful
Words for Writers, Poets & Dreamers

From Lazy R Softcovers, Spenard, Alaska
George G. Nagel, Editor
Fifth Issuance – December 2023
ISBN # 9798865151234

Abbreviations
adj. adjective; **adv.** adverb; **AKA** also known as;
BCE Before Common Era; **c.** century;
CE Common Era; **def.** definition;
e.g. *exempli gratia (for example)*;
esp. especially; **incl.** including or includes;
interj. interjection; **km** kilometers;
kph kilometers per hour; **m** meters;
mph miles per hour; **myth.** mythology;
NE northeast; **NW** northwest; **pl.** plural;
pop. population; **SE** southeast; **SW** southwest;
US United States; and **UK** United Kingdom.

Cover art: *Landscape – Scene from "Thanatopsis"*
by Asher B. Durand, 1850

Introduction

Dictionary of the Rare, Creative, and Beautiful is part dictionary, part portable, selective, and curated *encyclopedia*. This book offers a window into the breadth and depth of human experience and imagination, showcasing words with unique histories and meaning, or beauty of sound or appearance; others are esoteric and deep – or simply fascinatingly strange.

Within are words and beautiful names such as:
> *brontomantic, Denisovian, anacampserote, wildering, aprique, oneirogenic, circumundulate, chiromantic, tristisonous, umbratilous, obvolvent, Thulian pink, Thistlegorm, therocephalians, Fata Morgana Land, spumiferous, Panslavonian,* and *Muromian.*

Other categories of words, names, and terms are:
- <u>Placenames</u> (*Pillars of Hercules, Arabia Felix, Doon Edin, Mare Tenebrosum & Riphean Mountains*);
- <u>Zoology</u> (*quill pig, pink fairy armadillo & frantling*);
- <u>Astronomy</u> (*Eddington luminosity, Venusian, Silurian hypothesis, Jovian trojans & Kreutz sungrazers*);
- <u>Geopolitics</u> (*Perfidious Albion & Baltoscandia*);
- <u>History</u> (*Sahelian kingdoms, sunlit uplands & Groom of the Stool*);
- <u>Geometry</u> (*Penrose stairs & Villarceau circles*);
- <u>Anatomy</u> (*brain sand & frenulum*);
- <u>Archeology</u> (*Oldenburg Horn & Nebra sky disc*).

Plus <u>nautical</u>, <u>poetic</u>, and <u>literary</u> terms like:
    brave west winds & *naufragous*;
    person from Porlock & *the cavalier poets*;
    the Lost Generation & *Erewhonian*.

Also select <u>slang</u> words, such as: *tactical chunder,*
    snoutfair, molly wop, ghostshipping & *grundle.*

And interesting <u>phrases</u> like: *bring owls to Athens*;
    et in Arcadia ego; *dolce far niente*; and
    up the wooden hills to bedfordshire.

This is the third dictionary from Robin Devoe. The first – *Dictionary of the Strange, Curious, and Lovely* – is a collection of the 3500 "coolest" words in the English language. The second – *Epic English Words* – includes the best 10% or so of that 3500, and also interesting names and terms from diverse scientific, artistic, and literary fields. So *moonglade, nemorous & brontide*; and so too *Devonian, Muspelheim, Shambhala & Avalon* are included in *Epic English Words*. This book – *Dictionary of the Rare, Creative, and Beautiful* – is similar to *Epic English Words* except it includes almost all new entries. Each volume stands alone and if you like one, you will probably like all three.

The author hopes these books expand and enrichen the wordlore of English speakers and readers worldwide.

– Robin Devoe
Vale de Lune, Alaska – November Seven, MMXXIII

Book Notes

Select pronunciations and unusual plural forms are noted in (parentheses). [Bracketed] information appending entries may include part of speech, rarity, synonyms & antonyms, related words, etc.

Many entries' etymologies are also included. In the [bracketed] etymology information, foreign words are *italicized*, with meanings following, as in [Latin *Hibernia* Ireland]. These often include *etyma* (root words) and many also include *cognates* – words (often foreign) that have similar etymologies. Note that sometimes the feminine form of Latin words is used in etymologies. If an entry word itself is foreign (e.g., Mare Nubium) then the meaning is sometimes italicized instead, as in: [Latin *sea of clouds*]. Some entries include quotes (often poetical) showing word usage. Unattributed quotes are original example sentences.

Only one word in this dictionary – *soporadoratic* – was coined by the author. Some entries are noted as [very rare] or [obsolete] – these words may not be found even in large dictionaries and in some cases these selections are arguably not even "real" English words.

A

aardwolf (pl. *aardwolves*) a nocturnal, insect-eating mammal similar to a hyena and indigenous to southern Africa; [synonym: *earthwolf*]; [Afrikaans *aarde* (earth, soil)]

Aberdonian of or pertaining to Aberdeen, Scotland; a person from or living in Aberdeen; [adj. & noun]; [Medieval Latin *Aberdonia* Aberdeen]

abominate abominable; detested; to hate something with great vehemence; [adj. & verb]; [rare]

abyssal-hill province a region on the *abyssal plain* (the deep ocean floor) with many *abyssal hills* – small hills covering 30% of the ocean's floor

accrescent growing; increasing; in botany, growing larger even after flowering; [adj.]

accusatrix (pl. *accusatrices*) a female accuser; [rare noun]; [Latin]

acropolis a high point, often incl. a fortification, around which many ancient Greek cities were built; [Greek *ákros* extreme + *póli* city]

ad absurdum to the point of absurdity – used in Greek philosophy as an argument against something; [adverb]; [Latin, literally: *to absurdity*]

adieux farewells; [interj.]; [French *adieu* goodbye]

Adonic very handsome; pertaining to Adonis; [adj.]; [in Greek myth., *Adonis* was a particularly beautiful young man loved by Aphrodite]

aegis (pl. *aegides*) guidance; protection; [in Greek and Roman myth., a shield carried by Zeus and Athena]; "Under the *aegis* of France a

group of buffer states would be born."
– Nancy Barker, *Distaff Diplomacy*, 1967

aeolian dunes sand dunes formed from wind action
and appearing in five types: *linear, crescentic, star,
dome,* and *parabolic*; [noun]

aeolian processes the ways in which wind shapes
the surface of the Earth or other planets;
[geology]; [*Aeolus,* Greek god of the wind]

aerie or **eyrie** a bird of prey's nest; any high and
remote place; [noun]

affective haptics the study of devices that influence
the human emotional state through the sense of
touch; [German *haptisch* (relating to touch)]

affinitive closely connected; [adj.]; [noun: *affinity*];
[Catalan afí related]; "friends *affinitive*"

affluential a wealthy and well-connected person;
describing such a person; [noun & adj.];
[*affluent* + *influential*]

afflux the act of flowing towards or together;
a sudden upward flow of fluid; [noun];
[synonym: *affluxion*]

African dream root a South African herb held
sacred by the Xhosa people – used to induce
lucid dreams during shamanic initiations; [noun]

African sacred ibis a wading bird found in much of
Africa and part of the Middle East – linked to the
Egyptian god Thoth and locally extinct in Egypt

African superswell a region including the Southern
and Eastern African plateaux and the SE Atlantic
basin where a high degree of tectonic uplift
occurred, resulting in large areas of land relatively
high in altitude; [noun]

afterglow twilight after sunset; the moderately euphoric feeling sometimes felt after a pleasurable experience; [antonym: *foreglow*]; "Let my thoughts come to you, when I am gone, like the *afterglow* of sunset at the margin of starry silence." – Rabindranath Tagore, *Stray Birds*, 1916

afterworld the supposed world experienced after death; [noun]; "He dreamt of an *afterworld* in which she lived."

Age of Revolution, the historical period from the late-18th c. to the mid-19th c. marked by several notable revolutionary movements in Europe and the Americas, incl. the American (1765-1783) and the French (1789-1799) Revolutions; [historical]

aghast terrified; suddenly amazed; [adj.]

agitprop political propaganda distributed through drama, literature, art, etc. – esp. if communist; a specific instance of such; [noun]; [shortened from Department for *Agitation* and *Propaganda*]

agleam glowing with a soft light; [poetic adj.]; "London in the spring! Sunshine; the Thames *agleam* with silver ripples, singing as it flows; red sails!" – Frederic Isham, *Half a Chance*, 1909

aglimmer glimmering; shining; [poetic adj.]; [Swedish *glimma* (to gleam)]

agrosilviculture an agricultural technique that takes advantage of the interactive benefits of trees and shrubs combined with crops and/or livestock

airfaring flying in a plane or other aircraft; describing things that move at height through the air; [poetic adj.]; "He soon mastered the pilotage of the Venusians' *airfairing* craft."

aitchbone a cow's rump bone; [synonym: *edgebone*]; [Latin *natis* rump]

Albanian Intellectual Massacres the 1951 executions of 22 Albanian intellectuals ordered by Enver Hoxha, leader of Albania from 1944-1985; [historical]

alchemical or **alchemystical** pertaining to alchemy or transmutation; [adj.]

Alexandria's Genesis an urban legend and Internet myth purporting the existence of a rare human genetic mutation that results in purple eyes, shimmering pale skin, no body hair, and greater longevity

alfresco or **al fresco** outside; in the open air; [adj. & adv.]; [Italian *fresco* fresh]; "*alfresco* dining"

algedonic relating to both pleasure and pain; [adj.]; [Greek *álgos* pain + *idoní* pleasure]; "...the *algedonic* polarity of existence." – John Fowles, *The Magus*, 1965

Alice in Wonderland syndrome or **dysmetropsia** a condition that causes distortions of perception, esp. of vision; [noun]; [in Lewis Carroll's *Alice in Wonderland*, Alice seems to change size after drinking a potion and eating a cake]

allopreening preening, or grooming, another bird; the act of two birds grooming each other; [verb & noun]; [Ancient Greek *állos* other]

alpenglow a reddish glow upon alpine peaks during sunset or sunrise, esp. the former; [noun]

alpenhorn or **alphorn** a long wooden horn historically used by herders in the Alps to call cattle; [noun]

altiloquent bombastic or arrogant in speech; [rare adj.]; [Latin *altus* (high) + *loqui* (to speak)]

altocumulus (pl. *altocumuli*) a fleecy, mid-altitude cloud formation; [noun]; [Latin *altus* high + *cumulus* heaped]

amain forcefully; with strength; with much haste or at full-speed; [adverb]; [archaic & literary]

ambilevous being equally clumsy with both hands; having butterfingers; [rare adj.]; [antonym: *ambidextrous*]; [Latin *laevus* left]

American Bottom a floodplain of the Mississippi River in southern Illinois

American dollar princesses rich American women (often heiresses) who married a titled, European royal (often not rich) in effect exchanging cash for prestige – the term gained prominence in America's Gilded Age (1877-1900) during which there were about 450 such marriages; [historical]

American night or **day for night** a set of cinematic techniques used to make film shot during daylight look like night; [known in France as *nuit américaine* (American night) due to its formerly common use in Hollywood for low budget movies and westerns]

American pasqueflower or **prairie crocus** a plant native to much of western Canada and the United States – hairy stalks support lavender or white bell-shaped flowers

ammoniac relating to ammonia, esp. smelling like it; [adj.]; "The London train was crammed. Three gross Italians ... prepared themselves for sleep by taking off their boots. Their feet smelt strongly *ammoniac*, like a cage of mice long uncleaned."

— Aldous Huxley, *Limbo*, 1920

amnestic describing something that causes amnesia; [adj.]; [Ancient Greek *ámnēstos* (forgotten, forgetful)]

amorevolous affectionate; loving; [obsolete adj.]; [Italian *amorevole* loving]

amorphous without a clear form or shape; [adj.]; [Greek *morfí* shape]; "*amorphous* fog"

ampulla of Lorenzini (pl. *ampullae*) one of the electroreceptors that form a network of hydrogel-filled pores in the skin of cartilaginous fish; some fish use this network of sense organs to detect electrical stimuli from the muscle contractions of their prey; [noun]; [Stefano *Lorenzini*, 17th c. Italian ichthyologist]

anacampserote (ana-KAMP-sir-oat) a thing that can restore a romantic relationship thought to be forever lost; [very rare]; [the botanical genus *Anacampseros* is an ancient name for herbs thought to restore a *lost love*]; [Ancient Greek *anakámptō* (turn back)]; "The romantic trip to the Cantabrian Coast seemed an ideal *anacampserote* to revivify their most cherished dreams together."

anaclastic produced by the refraction of light, as seen through water; refracting; breaking the rectilinear course of light; [adj.]; "*anaclastic* distortions"

anapest in poetry, a metrical foot with two unstressed & one stressed syllable or two short & one long syllable; a line of poetry that uses this meter; [noun]; [adj. *anapestic*]; [synonym: *antidactylus*]; [Ancient Greek *aná* (back) + *paíō* (I strike)]; "*anapestic* verse"

Anapilis a very tall & steep fictional mountain and place of the afterlife in Lithuanian myth.; [Lithuanian *ana* that + *pilis* castle]

Andalusian independentist conspiracy an alleged plot led by a duke and a marquis in 1641 for *Andalusia* to secede from Spain, then ruled by *King Phillip IV* – many details of this failed conspiracy remain unclear; [historical]

androsphinx (pl. *androsphinges*) a male *sphinx* – a mythological creature with a human head and a lion's body; [Ancient Greek *andrós* man]; "*Androsphinges* possess a certain feline beauty, certes, but the attached human head seems incongruitous and ruins the overall effect."

angle of repose the steepest angle at which granular material can settle and not be subject to gravitational movement; e.g., wet sand has an *angle of repose* of 45 degrees; [rare figurative usage]; "His *angle of repose* had now dropped to 34 degrees, equal to that of dry sand."

anguiped or **anguipedal** having serpents in place of feet or legs, such as the snake-footed giants of Greek myth.; [adj.]; [Latin *anguis* snake + *pedālis* foot]

anharmonic or **inharmonic** discordant; not harmonic; [adj.]; [Ancient Greek *an-* (not, without)]; [Latin *harmonia* harmony]

anorchous without testes; [rare adj.]; [synonym: *anorchic*]; [Ancient Greek *órkhis* (testicle, orchid)]; "The captive men were tortured, pitiful, hopeless, and *anorchous.*"

anthemic in music, like an anthem; provoking; exciting; rousing; [adj.]; "They soon broke into song, spirited and *anthemic*."

anthimeria or **antimaria** a rhetorical device wherein one part of speech is used as another – often using a noun as if it were a verb; [synonym: *verbing*]; [Ancient Greek *antí* opposite + *méros* part]; [Example: "*Grace* me no grace, nor *uncle* me no uncle" – Shakespeare]

apanthropy an aversion to human company; a love of solitude; [noun]

apeirogon (AH-peer-oh-gone) a theoretical polygon with an infinite number of sides; [geometry]; [rare noun]; [Greek *ápeiros* infinite]

apeiron (pl. *apeira*) the unlimited and indefinite origin or first principle of all matter, esp. as conceived by the Ancient Greek philosopher Anaximander; [French *apeiron* infinity]

aphantasia a rare condition where an *aphantasiac* cannot visualize imagery or lacks a *mind's eye*; [Latin *phantasia* (idea, fantasy)]

Aphrodite ancient Greek goddess associated with love, beauty, and procreation – she was born from sea foam; [Greek *aphros* foam]

aplomb composure; self-confidence; [French]; "His *aplomb* was innate and complete."

Apollonian circles in geometry, two sets of circles that intersect each other at right angles; [noun]; [Greek geometer *Apollonius* of Perga]

Apollyon or **Abaddon** an angel described in the *Book of Revelations* as the king of the locusts; a bottomless pit mentioned in the Bible; [Greek *apóllymi* (to destroy)]

apperception the human mind's recognition of itself; self-consciousness; mental perception

après moi, le déluge used to indicate indifference
to a disaster after one's death, or to indicate
one's own importance in maintaining order;
[phrase]; [French, literally: *after me, the flood*];
[attributed to French King Louis XV]; "Depose me
and civilization will fall! *Après moi, le déluge*."

aprique sunny; sun-loving; [adj.]; [archaic &
very rare]; [Latin *aprīca* sunny]

aqueous watery; made up of mostly water; [adj.];
"*Aqueous* fruits helped extend their water supply."

aquiline like an eagle; [adj.]; [Latin *aquila* eagle];
"an *aquiline* visage"

aquiver quivering; in an excited state; [adj.]

Arabia Felix an old name for the southwestern
portion of the Arabian Peninsula – what is now
mostly Yemen; [Latin *Fertile Arabia*]

archaeolatry worshipping or revering ancient times;
[noun]

archangelic or **archangelical** like or pertaining to an
archangel – a leader of angels; [adj.]; [Portuguese
arqui- highest]; "*archangelic* powers"

architectonics the science of architecture; [noun]

arfarfanarf very intoxicated; [adj.]; [archaic & rare];
[UK slang]

Argo Navis an obsolete constellation in the
southern sky; [*Argo* – the ship that sailed in
pursuit of the Golden Fleece in Greek myth.]

Argus Panoptes a many-eyed giant; [Greek myth.]

aria a musical solo usually accompanied by an
orchestra; [Greek *aéras* (air, wind)]

Aristotle's lantern a sea urchin's chewing organ or
jaws; [noun]; [from Aristotle's *History of Animals*
in which he describes the organ as looking like

a horn *lantern* with the panes of horn removed]

as rare as rocking horse sh*t so rare as to almost never (or absolutely never) occur; [UK slang]

ascendant rising; surpassing; [adj.]; "an *ascendant* lifepath"

ashen light a subtle glow claimed to be seen (from Earth) on the night side of Venus – not confirmed scientifically, but hypothesized to be due to the presence of lightning

ashimmer shimmering; shining intermittently; [rare adj.]; "The sun had set the peak of Olympus all *ashimmer*." – H. N. Brailsford, *The Broom of the War-God*, 1898

aspirant a person that aspires to some ambition; pursuing advancement; [noun & adj.]

astragalomancy predicting the future by means of dice, esp. dice made of bones; [Greek *ostó* bone]

astral plane, **astral realm**, or **astral world** a plane of existence, postulated by several philosophies and mystery religions, inhabited by various types of immaterial beings – the plane is sometimes conflated with heaven; [noun]

astronomical twilight when the sun is between 12 and 18 degrees below the horizon after dusk or before dawn; after *astronomical twilight* in the evening, the sun does not illuminate the sky at all and *night* officially begins

astrophile a person who loves the stars; [rare noun]

astrotheology or **astral mysticism** the worship of stars and other heavenly bodies or the association of deities with same

asunder into separate parts, as torn *asunder*; [adverb]; [synonym: *in twain*]; "What therefore

God hath joined together, let not man put *asunder.*" – Jesus

athwart across or over; at an unparallel angle; [adverb & preposition]; [synonym: *transversely*]; "But oh! that deep romantic chasm which slanted Down the green hill *athwart* a cedarn cover!" – Samuel Taylor Coleridge, *Kubla Khan*, 1797

attar an essential oil, usually fragrant, obtained from a flower; [noun]; [Persian *'atr* (scent, perfume)]; "I bequeath to you my literary work. Useless though these might be commercially, they are the *attar*-drops distilled from the long and futile ebullience of my life." – Xavier Herbert, *Capricornia*

auberge (ow-BEARJ) an inn or hostel; [French]

Audenesque akin to the Anglo-American poet W. H. *Auden* (1907-1973); characterized by the exploration of the relationship between a person and the impersonal world of nature; [adj.]

augury supposed knowledge of the future based on animals' behavior; omen; prophecy; an event supposed to be indicative of an important future event; [noun]; [synonym: *portent*]; [verb: *augur*]; [Turkish *uğur* (luck, fortune)]; "We defy *augury*; there's a special providence in the fall of a sparrow." – Shakespeare, *Hamlet*, 1602

august noble; majestic; [adj.]; "*august* dreams"

aureate gold-colored; shining golden; [adj.]; [rare synonym: *aurelian*]

auriferous producing, containing, or bearing gold; [adj.]; [synonym: *aurific*]; [Latin *aurifer* gold-bearing]

aurify to turn to gold; [rare verb]

auriphrygiate decorated with gold; [rare adj.];
  [Aragonese, Finnish, Spanish, Italian *oro* gold]
aurorean like, or of, the dawn; [poetic adj.];
  "Their lips touch'd not, but had not bade adieu,
  As if disjoined by soft-handed slumber,
  And ready still past kisses to outnumber
  At tender eye-dawn of *aurorean* love:"
  – John Keats, *Ode to Psyche*, 1820
avifauna the birds living in a region; [adj. *avifaunal*]
axis mundi or **cosmic axis** the axis of Earth that
  extends between the celestial poles; figuratively,
  any mythological representation of a connection
  between Heaven and Earth
Aztec two-step or **Montezuma's revenge** diarrhea
  while travelling, esp. if in Mexico or Central
  America; [Emperor *Moctezuma* II – killed in 1520
  during the Spanish conquest of the Aztec Empire]

B

Baba Yaga a supernatural being in Slavic folklore
  that appears as a deformed, ferocious woman;
  [Polish *babunia* (little grandmother)]; [Czech
  jezinka (evil forest fairy)]
Babylonian star catalogues collated stellar
  observations that include some modern
  constellations – the oldest of the catalogues
  was compiled in the 12th century BCE
balconic related to balconies; occurring on a
  balcony; [adj.]; "She relished their hungry, brief,
  and almost entirely *balconic* tryst."
Balkan crested newt an amphibian native to
  Southeastern Europe
balletic relating to, akin to, or suitable for ballet;

[adj.]; *"balletic* maneuvers"

ballhooter a logger who rolls large logs down steep slopes; [noun]

Baltia or **Abalus** a mythic island of northern Europe mentioned in ancient Greco-Roman geography – supposedly amber would wash ashore in spring

Baltoscandia a concept of cooperation between the Nordic & Baltic countries of Denmark, Estonia, Finland, Iceland, Latvia, Lithuania, Norway, and Sweden – first proposed in 1928; [Lithuanian *baltas* white]; [Latin *balteus* belt]

Baltis an ancient Arabian goddess associated with the planet *Venus* and equivalent to the Babylonian goddess *Ishtar*

banjaxed broken; destroyed; shattered; tired; spent; sleepy; knackered; [adj.]; [UK slang]

barbaresque having a barbaric artistic style; relating to the *Barbary* area of North Africa; [adj.]

barbatulous having a very small beard; [adj.]; [archaic & very rare]; [Latin *barbatulus* (a little beard)]

bardiglio veined Italian marble with three main types: *common*, *dark*, and *floral*; [noun]

baronial relating to barons; fit for a baron; large and impressive; stately; [adj.]; *"baronial* lodging"

bastardry the state of being illegitimate offspring; the unpleasant actions of a bad person; [noun]

batfowling catching birds by scaring them awake at night whereupon they fly toward a nearby fire and may be caught in nets; [noun: *bat-fowler*]

beach moonflower or **sea moonflower** a widespread, perennial plant with white flowers that open at night

becarpeted covered as with a carpet; [poetic adj.]; "a meadow in delicate flora *becarpeted*"

becastled having castles; secured by a castle or castles; [adj.]; "The *becastled* lands of that august monarch's expansive realm lay in ruins."

becharm to charm; to hold spellbound; [verb]; "...the *becharmed* crew maintaining the profoundest silence, as the head-bent waves hammered..." – Herman Melville, *Moby-Dick*, 1851

bedarken to make dark or dim; [poetic verb]

bedewed covered with dew; moistened as if with dew; [literary adj.];
"...moistened and *bedewed* with Pleasures." – John Keats, *Letter to Fanny Brawne*, 1819
"'What makes you think that?' I asked, handkerchiefing my upper slopes, which had become considerably *bedewed*. I didn't like this line of talk at all." – P. G. Wodehouse, 1960

bedlamite a lunatic; [noun]; [*Bedlam*, an alternative name for the Bethlem Royal Hospital, a psychiatric hospital in London]

bedwork work done in bed or done with great ease; [noun]; [archaic & rare]

befoam to cover or partially cover with foam; [rare verb]; "*befoaming* seas"

begirdle to encircle; [verb]

beleaguered beseiged; surrounded by an enemy or by difficulties; beset by trouble; [adj.]

belike to resemble; to like; likely or probable; perhaps; probably; [verb & adverb]

belletristic like literature mainly valued for aesthetic properties; appreciated for beauty or artistic value rather than for content; [adj.]; "*belletristic* verse"

Bellona the ancient Roman goddess of war –
sister of Mars and known for her bloodlust and
madness in battle; a brave and vigorous woman;
[Latin *bellum* war]

belly god or **belly-god** a food lover; a glutton;
[rare noun]

Belphegor in the Christian tradition, the chief
demon of the deadly sin *Sloth*; seduces people
by suggesting ingenious inventions to make
them rich

belvedere a turret or similar structure that offers a
commanding view; [Italian, literally: *fair view*]

bemonster to make hideous or like a monster;
[verb]; [adj. *bemonstered*];
"Thou changed and self-cover'd thing, for shame!
Bemonster not thy feature!"
– Shakespeare, *King Lear*, 1608

benighted lacking knowledge; unenlightened; [adj.];
[figurative]

bereft deprived or robbed of; lacking; feeling
sadness at the loss of someone; [adj.]; "Thrown
on the wide world, doomed to wander and roam,
Bereft of his parents, *bereft* of a home."
– Charles Dickens, *Bleak House*, 1853

bespoke custom made; [adj.]; [UK]

bestial like a beast; savage; [adj.]

bête noire something (or someone) that is
particularly loathed or avoided; [noun];
[French, literally: *black beast*]

Betteridge's law of headlines this law states that
any news headline that ends in a question mark
can be answered in the negative; if the publishers
were confident of a positive answer, they would

have presented the headline as a statement of truth; [Ian *Betteridge*, British tech journalist]

bibliobibuli (pl. only) people who read too much; [Ancient Greek *biblíon* (book) + Latin *bibulus* (fond of drink) – coined in 1957 by H. L. Mencken]

bibliophage or **bibliophagist** a bookworm; a great lover of reading books; [noun]; [Ancient Greek *biblíon* (book) + *phageîn* (to eat)]

bicrescentic having the form of a double crescent, esp. a pair of crescent moons joined in the middle; [rare adj.]

bicorporal having two bodies; [rare adj.]

Big Rip, the in physical cosmology, the hypothesis that eventually the expansion of the universe will rip apart all matter until the distances between subatomic particles become infinite

biophilia a love of nature and living things; [noun]

Birches, The a village in Northern Ireland; [others include: *Blackskull, Downpatrick, Groomsport, Mazetown, Moneyglass, Moss-Side* & *Silverbridge*]

birdlore ornithology; the knowledge or study of birds; [noun]; "an expert in *birdlore*"

bitchcraft the skills and knowledge employed in being a bitch; "Hers was a finely-tuned species of *bitchcraft*, honed over decades sad & sour."

Black Norwegian Elkhound a small breed of hunting dog – very rare outside Scandinavia

blackguard or **blaggard** a scoundrel; a man that is untrustworthy; [noun]

blackwash a campaign to villify something or someone; to villianize; [noun & verb]; [antonym: *whitewash*]

blamestorm a group effort to assign blame for, or discover the cause of, some failure; to engage in a *blamestorm*; [noun & verb]

blandiloquent speaking in a gentle, agreeable, or flattering way; [rare adj.]; [archaic noun: *blandiloquence*]; [Latin *blanda* (agreeable, flattering)]; [Portuguese *brando* gentle]

Blattnerphone an early magentic audio recording device developed in the late 1920's; used in 1939 to record British Prime Minister Neville Chamberlain announcing the start of WWII; [Ludvig *Blattner*, German-born inventor]

blinkered wearing blinders; unable to see obvious happenings around oneself; [adj.]

bloodstroke an attack with a weapon that draws blood, esp. a significant amount of blood; "Cleaving the air with *bloodstroke* upon *bloodstroke*, Jarl made his bitter steel sing." – Hugh Cook, *Witchlord & Weaponmaster*, 2006

blue hour the period of twilight (either morning or evening) when the sun is roughly 4-8 degrees below the horizon and the sky takes on various shades of blue; [noun]; [synonym: *gloaming*]

bogart a selfish or arrogant person; to selfishly take or hog something, esp. a marijuana cigarette; to obtain something in a bullying fashion; to act like a tough guy; [noun & verb]; [American slang]

bogosity being bogus; being fake or undesirable; "...the inflated *bogosity* of tourist hotel food..." – Ian Fleming, *Thunderball*, 1961

bolt from the blue a total surprise; [noun]; [synonym: *deus ex machina*]; [from seeming to come from out of nowhere, as would lightning on a clear day]

Boltzmann brain a hypothetical entity that develops and becomes self-aware due to random changes in spacetime; [noun]; [19th c. Austrian physicist Ludwig *Boltzmann*]

bombazine a twilled or corded fabric of silk, wool, or cotton, the latter being dyed black; [noun]; [Latin *bombȳx* silkworm]

bone-eating snot flower worm a creature with worm-like characteristics that subsists on dead minke whales; [Greek & Latin *Osedax mucofloris,* literally: *snot-flower bone-eater*]

bonhomie a friendly and pleasant manner; an affable disposition; [noun]; [adj. *bonhomous*]

bonk to hit something; to have sex; to experience sudden fatigue in an endurance sport; [verb]; "Zude, I totally *bonked* on that last uphill."

bookcraft authorship; literary talent; [archaic noun]

Boring Billion, **the** or **the Mid Proterozoic** the time period .8 to 1.8 billion years ago during which the Earth's geology and climate were relatively stable, with slow biological evolution

born to the purple born and raised rich and privileged or in a royal family; [a room in the imperial *Great Palace of Constantinople* where reigning empresses gave birth was lined with *porphyry,* an expensive purplish rock]

bornhardt a steep, dome-shaped, bare rock at least 100 feet high; similar to an *inselberg,* but not necessarily isolated; [Wilhelm *Bornhardt,* 19th c. explorer of German East Africa]

boscage an area with trees or shrubs; a grove

bourasque a tempest or storm; [archaic]; [French]

brachistochrone curve in mathematics, the curve defining the fastest descent between two given points when frictionless and under the influence of a uniform gravitational field; [Ancient Greek *brákhistos khrónos* (shortest time)]

brain sand or **corpora arenacea** calcified concretions of various minerals that increasingly form in the brain with age, esp. in the pineal gland – this gland produces melatonin and regulates sleep, but the purpose, if any, of *brain sand* is unknown; [Latin *arēna* sand]

Brandolini's law or **the BS asymmetry principle** this Internet adage coined in 2013 states that: "The amount of energy needed to refute bullsh*t is an order of magnitude bigger than that needed to produce it."; [Alberto *Brandolini*, Italian programmer]

brave west winds the robust and relatively persistent westerly winds that blow across the oceans in temperate latitudes; [nautical]

bregma (pl. *bregmata*) an anatomical point atop the skull where the frontal bone meets the parietal bones; [adj. *bregmoid*]

bring owls to Athens to do something pointless or superfluous; to bring a thing (or an idea) to a location where the thing is already commonplace or not needed; [synonym: *carry coals to Newcastle*]

Britomartis a mountain nymph and Cretan goddess of mountains and hunting; [Greek myth.]

Brobdingnagian huge; much larger than is typical; [*Brobdingnag*, a land of giants in Jonathan Swift's *Gulliver's Travels*]

brogue a dialectal accent, esp. if prominent – often used to describe the English speech of persons from Ireland or Scotland; a sturdy Oxford shoe; "A mellifluent Irish *brogue* lent his every word an undeniable charm."

brontomancy telling the future or revealing secrets by listening to thunder; [very rare noun]; [adj. *brontomantic*]; "*brontomantic* prophecies"

brood patch a featherless area on birds that helps to transfer heat to eggs during incubation

brown trouser moment a terrifying moment, esp. if also a surprise; [UK slang]

brownshort pooping one's trousers, shorts, or underwear due to a very unpleasant surprise; [usually figurative]; "Upon first hearing of your betrothal to my sister, I nearly *brownshorted*."

brumation a type of stasis similar to hibernation undergone by some species of reptile; [Latin *brūma* (winter solstice)]; "The archeologist was careful not to disturb any *brumating* bearded dragons during the midwinter dig."

brutalist architecture a style developed in the UK during the 1950s – characterized by minimalist construction, bare building materials, and non-decorative designs

Brythonic a Celtic language; relating to the Brythonic group of Celtic languages; [noun & adj.]; [synonym: *Brittonic*]; "*Brythonic* placenames"

bulbaceous or **bulbous** shaped like a bulb; bloated; overweight and round; [adj.]

bushcraft the skills needed for survival in a given natural environment, esp. in wilderness

bussin or **bussin'** describing something very good, awesome, or cool; [adj. or interjection]; [American slang]

Byronics behavior that is in the style (or intending to be in the style) of Lord Byron; *Byronic* actions or speech; [noun]; "Later in the party, even his most tolerant friends tired of his inebriate *Byronics*."

C

C-suite the group of lead officers in a company, often with the word chief in their titles; [*C* in *chief* + *suite*]; "The *C-suite* went totally rogue, not even pretending to be beholden to the Board."

cacophony discordant sounds; dissonance; [adj. *cacophonic*]; [antonym: *euphony*]; [Greek *kakós* evil]

cadaverous looking like a corpse or a dead body; pale and lifeless; [adj.]; "Mrs. Spoker ... was as inclement in demeanour as she was *cadaverous* in aspect." – Ben Travers, *A Cuckoo in the Nest*, 1925

caesious having a light blue color; lavender in color; pale blue with some grey; [rare adj.]; [Latin *caelum* sky]

calamistrate to curl the hair, esp. with a curling iron; [rare verb]; [Latin *calamistrum* (curling iron)]

Caligulan or **Caligulean** pertaining to Caligula; savagely cruel or tyrannical; [rare adj.]; [*Caligula*, 1st c. Roman emperor who was cruel, extravagant, sexually perverse, and mentally unsound]

Callitrix or **Satyrus** a mythological ape-like creature that always bore twins, loving one and hating the other; [medieval folklore]

calvaria the bony dome of the skull; [noun]; [Spanish *calavera* (skull, libertine)]

Cambrian explosion the rapid increase in the number of animal *phyla* during the Cambrian period over 500 million years BCE; the rapid creation or appearance of anything; "Post-Prohibition, the city experienced a *Cambrian explosion* of drinking establishments."

Camelopardalis a constellation somewhat resembling a giraffe; [Ancient Greek *kámēlos* (camel) + *párdalis* (leopard) because long neck like camel and spotted like leopard]

Camelot the castle and court of the legendary King Arthur; [adj. *Camelotian*]; [possibly from *Cavalon* – a place name that itself may be an alteration of *Avalon*]

camoufleur a person that utilizes camouflage or disguises or hides their physical presence; [rare]; "An incorrigible *camoufleur,* George would hide in the foliage dressed in full camouflage and challenge me to find him on my walk home."

campcraft skills employed during camping expeditions, such as *axe handling* or *tracking*

canaille (KUH-nigh) the lowest class; the rabble; [French]

Cantabrian Mountains or **Cantabrian Range** a 300-kilometer-long mountain range across northern Spain and along the Cantabrian Sea; [Cantabrian is possibly from Celtic for *people who live in the rocks*]

canterbury an often decorative, usually wooden rack for periodicals or other papers; [noun]; [*Canterbury*, the cathedral city in England]

caper-cutting caperous; frolicksome; [adj.]; [noun: *caper cutting*]; [*caper*: a playful leap, esp. while dancing]

Capraesque similar to or reminiscent of the films of Frank Capra, American director of 36 feature-length films including *It Happened One Night* (1934) and *It's a Wonderful Life* (1946); [adj.]

Capri or **Capri blue** a sky blue color between cyan & azure; [noun]

caprice an impulsive action or notion, esp. if seeming to lack logical motivation; a short-lived romance; an unpredictable change; [Italian *capriccio* (whim, fancy)]; "we... entered a fantastic world...in which the narrow... road rose and fell and curved with an almost sentient and purposeful *caprice* amidst the tenantless green peaks and half-deserted valleys" – H.P. Lovecraft, *The Whisperer in Darkness*, 1931

Captain Alfred Bulltop Stormalong a New England folk hero said to be a 30-feet tall sailor

carcass-roofing transporting a freshly killed animal, often a deer, on the roof of a car; [verb & adj.]; [very rare]; [American slang]; "Who were we to judge these *carcass-roofing* Arkansans?"

Carcosa a mysterious city hinted at in Ambrose Bierce's 1886 short story *An Inhabitant of Carcosa* – several subsequent writers used the name Carcosa or referenced it

cartomantic pertaining to fortune telling with a deck of cards, esp. tarot cards; [adj.]; [noun: *cartomancy*]; "*cartomantic* advice"

Casper's Dictum the proposed ratio of the time until a body putrefies in air, water, and earth – 1:2:8;

[Johann Ludvig *Casper*, 19th c. German forensic scientist]

Caspian naked-fingered gecko a gecko native to parts of Russia and the Republic of Georgia

Caspian snowcock a wary bird with a desolate whistling song that breeds at an altitude of 1800-3000 meters and is endemic to eastern Turkey, northern Iran, Armenia, and Azerbaijan

catacomb an underground system of tunnels and rooms designed to inter the dead, as in Paris or ancient Rome; [adj. *catacombic*]; [Spanish *tumba* tomb]

catacoustics the science of reflected sound; [archaic noun]; [Ancient Greek *katá* against]

catamenia menstrual flow; [noun]; [from Ancient Greek for *monthly*]

catapeltic or **catapultic** relating to a catapult; resembling the motion of a catapult; [adj.]; [Ancient Greek *katá* (against, down) + *pállō* (to poise a missile before throwing)]

Catatumbo Lightning a thunderstorm recurring an average of 150 nights per year over the Catatumbo River in Venezuela that produces up to 40 lightning flashes per minute; [Bari language *catatumbo* (house of thunder)]

caterwaul to cry like a cat in heat; to engage in a noisy argument; [verb]; [Middle English *cater* (cat) + *wrawen* (to anger)]

catharsis (pl. *catharses*) a release of emotional tension, esp. while watching a dramatic production and esp. if the release results in purified emotions; [noun]; [adj. *cathartic*]; [Ancient Greek *kátharsis* (cleansing, purging)]

Caucasity stereotypical behavior of racially white people, esp. if arrogant or entitled; the state of being racially Caucasian; [very rare noun]; [first definition: *Caucasian* + *audacity*]; "She deemed the overt *Caucasity* of the nouveau riche Europeans nauseating."

cavalier poets a school of 17th c. English poetry supported by *King Charles I* that celebrated nature, beauty, love, honor, drinking, good fellowship, and glorification of the King – notable cavalier poets include Richard Lovelace and Sir John Suckling; [literary & historical]

cavernicolous living in caves; [rare adj.]; "Dragons are the most feared of *cavernicolous* beasts."

celerity speed; swiftness; [noun]; [Italian *celere* quick]; "She moved with an agile *celerity*..."

celestine celestial; like the heavens; a resident of Heaven, such as an angel; [adj. & noun]; [rare]; [Spanish *cielo* (sky, heaven)]; "*celestine* purity"

Center of the World an American town in the midwestern state of Ohio

centaur in Greek myth. a beast with a horse's body and a man's head and torso; a chess team comprised of a human and a computer; [feminine *centauress*]; [adj. *centaurian*]; [first def. synonym: *hippocentaur*]

centiday the timespan of 1/100th of a day – 14 minutes and 24 seconds; [nonstandard time unit]

centuried very old; having existed or endured centuries; [adj.]; "*centuried* castles"

cephalic vein a *superficial* (or close to the skin) vein in the arm; [*cephalic* means "relating to the head"

– this particular, unusual usage resulted from a mistranslation of Arabic *al-kífal* (outer)]

cermet a composite of ceramic and metal – ceramic has high temperature resistance and hardness, while metal has a higher plastic deformation range than ceramic; [**cer**amic + **met**al]

ceromancy predicting the future by pouring wax into water and interpreting the bubbles thereof; [Ancient Greek *kērós* beeswax]

certes certainly; indeed; [archaic adverb]; [synonym: *verily*]; "Here, *certes*, was no lost soul, but one who had gone joyfully to meet her Lord." – John Buchan, *The Outgoing of the Tide*, 1902

chakravartin an ideal, benevolent ruler of the entire world; [Indian religion & myth.]; [Sanskrit *wheel-turner*]

Chamrosh a bird with a wolf's body and an eagle's wings that lives atop Mount Alborz beneath the *soma tree* and spreads all kinds of seeds across the Earth; [Persian myth.]

charismatic megafauna large wild animals that are loved by many, sometimes used to further environmentalist goals, and often hold symbolic value – examples include lions, elephants, giant pandas, gorillas, blue whales, and eastern imperial eagles

charm collective term for a flock of finch or goldfinch; "He startled a *charm* of finch..."

chasmic like a chasm; very wide and deep; [adj.]; "*chasmic* separation"

Chatham House Rule a rule stating that anyone who comes to a meeting is free to disclose anything about what was said, but may not disclose who made any particular comment; used by the *Bilderberg Group* and sometimes by the *European Central Bank*; [named after the London headquarters of the *Royal Institute of International Affairs*]

chatter marks in carpentry, indents in wood left by errant hammer strokes; [noun]; [very rare antonym: *Dutch rose* (imprint around a set nail)]

cheilion either area on the human mouth where the upper and lower lips meet; either corner of the mouth; [Greek *cheílos* lip]

cherub (pl. *cherubim*) a winged attendant of God ranked just below *seraphim* in the order of angels; a particularly angelic person, esp. such a child; [noun]; [adj. *cherubic*]; [Portuguese *querubim* cherub]

chevron a formation of geese in flight; [rare noun]; [French *chevron* rafter]

chiromancy fortune telling by reading lines in the hand; [noun]; [adj. *chiromantic*]; [synonym: *palmistry*]; "*chiromantic* predictions"

chivalresque characteristic of *chivalry*, esp. honorable conduct by men towards women; [adj.]; [synonyms: *chivalrous* & *gallant*]

choleric expressing anger; [adj.]; [Old French *colerique* bilious]; "*choleric* speech"

chronophagous time-consuming; [rare adj.]; [noun: *chronophage*]; "idle, *chronophagous* chatter"

chunder vomit, esp. due to excess drink; to vomit; [noun & verb]; [UK & Australian slang]; [perhaps from the expression *watch under* – shouted when British prisoners en route to

Australia became nauseated from turbulent seas];
"I come from a land down under
Where beer does flow and men *chunder*
Can't you hear, can't you hear the thunder?"
– Men at Work, *Down Under*, 1980

chunter or **chunner** to complain vocally, esp. in a constant, low, often incomprehensible manner; to grumble; [verb]

chyron the graphics or text often seen at the bottom of a TV screen, esp. on news channels; [the *Chyron* Corporation generates many such graphics]

circle of danger or **blood bubble** the imaginary circle (roughly 10 feet in radius) around a worker that is using tools to build a trail within which it is dangerous for others to be

circumambulate to walk around something, esp. in a circle or for a religious purpose; [verb]; [adj. *circumambulatory*]; "*Circumambulate* the city of a dreamy Sabbath afternoon."
– Herman Melville, *Moby-Dick*, 1851

circumboreal throughout Earth's far northern regions; of or pertaining to the vast forest regions in the northern areas of Eurasia and North America; [adj.]

circumferentially in an encircling manner; around the surface of a round or spherical object; so as to surround or encircle; [adverb]

circumfluent flowing around; surrounding like a fluid; "The deep, *circumfluent* waves."
– Homer, the *Odyssey*

circumgyratory moving in a circle; turning round; [adj.]; [Latin *gȳrus* circle]; "*circumgyratory* currents"

circumlocutionary communicated in a roundabout way; evasive in speech; [adj.]; "His *circumlocutionary* explanation did little to advance his claim of innocence."

circumstanced in a given situation or set of circumstances; [adj.]; "It might have been supposed that, given a girl rapidly becoming good-looking, comfortably *circumstanced*, and for the first time in her life commanding ready money, she would go and make a fool of herself by dress."
– Thomas Hardy, *The Mayor of Casterbridge*, 1886

circumundulate to flow around in waves or in a wave-like motion; [verb]; [noun: *circumundulation*]; [Latin *unda* wave]

circumvolution something sinuous or winding; the act of rotating or revolving around something, esp. an axis; [noun]; [verb: *circumvolute*]; "The *circumvolution* of his intricate & meandering mind was, eventually, a meet recompense for considerable patience."

cirrus intortus cirrus clouds that are curved in a random pattern; [rare noun]; [Latin *intorta* contorted]

cirrus uncinus cloud a high-altitude cloud formation, usually sparse and thin; [synonym: *mares' tails*]; [Latin *curly hooks*]

cisatlantic or **Cisatlantic** located on the same side of the Atlantic Ocean; [adj.]; "Both preferred a continental to an insular manner of life, a *cisatlantic* to a transatlantic place of residence."
– James Joyce, *Ulysses*, 1922

civil twilight when the Sun is between zero and six degrees below the horizon – during this period artificial light is unnecessary because enough natural light remains; [the sky is darker during *nautical twilight* and *astronomical twilight*]

claggy sticky; [adj.]; [synonym: *agglutinative*]; [Swedish *klägg* gunk]; "*claggy* mud"

clairalience the supposed paranormal ability to gain psychic knowledge through the sense of smell; [very rare noun]; [synonyms: *clairscent* & *clairolfaction*]

clairsentient exhibiting or relating to *clairsentience* or extra-sensory perception; one who has such an ability; [adj. & noun]; [rare]; [French *clair* clear]; "Her detailed prognostications were so accurate, they appeared in hindsight almost perfectly *clairsentient*."

cliffed coast or **abrasion coast** a type of coastline where waves have formed steep, or even precipitous, cliffs; [antonym: *alluvial coast*]

climacteric crucial; decisive; relating to any of several supposedly critical years (or turning points) in a person's life; *climactic* – pertaining to a climax; a crucial stage or turning point; [adj. & noun]; [Ancient Greek *klīmax* (ladder, staircase)]; "During those *climacteric* months soon after his 22nd birthday..."

clinchpoop or **clenchpoop** an uneducated person with bad manners; [obsolete noun]

cloud-born born from a cloud; having divine, or highly privileged, parentage; [adj.]; "These coastal elites, strutting about as if *cloud-born*..."

cloudborne transported by clouds; [adj]

cloudburst a heavy and sudden rainstorm; [noun]; [synonym: *cloudbust*]

cloud-kissing touching the clouds; lofty; [rare adj.]

cloudland a land of fantasy; a dreamland; [noun]

cloudwashed swept, covered, or shadowed by clouds; [adj.]; *"cloudwashed* landscape"

clown show a large political or administrative mess; a ridiculous, very disorganized, or chaotic scene; an organizational process or an event that comes off very poorly either due to bad luck or poor management; [rare noun]; [American slang]; "The gubernatorial administration was incompetent and mockable from the onset, but soon devolved into a total *clown show."*

clumperton a clownish or clumsy oaf; [noun]

cockchafer or **doodlebug** a flying European beetle

cocksman (pl. *cocksmen*) a sexually talented (or just promiscuous) human male; [rare noun]; [slang]

coco de mer a tall palm tree native to the Seychelles, or the nut therefrom; [French *nut of the sea*]

cognomen (pl. *cognomina*) last name; surname; nickname; [noun]; [literary or humorous]; [Latin]; "Hyphenated *cognomina* usually annoyed him, but in her case he found it charming."

cold reading a collection of techniques used by psychics to obtain information about people (with no prior knowledge) based on body language, clothing, hair style, manner of speech, etc.; [antonym: *hot reading*]

colorable seemingly true but not; specious; in law, fake, misleading, or not what is claimed to be

comatulid a free-swimming, stalkless marine animal with ten feathery appendages that lives on the seafloor, both shallow and deep; [synonym: *feather star*]

connubial of or pertaining to marriage; [adj.]; [synonym: *conjugal*]; [Italian *connubi* marriages]; "*connubial* familiarity"

conspiracy collective term for a group of lemurs

Conspiracy of Fire Cells a modern Greek anarchist urban guerrilla organization critical of capitalist society

contravallation a line of fortifications near a besieged city built by the attackers for tactical advantage; [archaic synonym: *countervallation*]

contumelious rudely expressing disdain or insolence; [adj.]; [archaic & literary]; [synonyms: *insolent* & *disdainful*]; [Italian *contumelia* insult]

conundrum (pl. *conundra*) a problem with seemingly no solution; a difficult riddle; a hard decision that must be made; "beset by seemingly unsolvable *conundra*"

convocation collective term for a group of eagles

Copernican pertaining to Renaissance astronomer Nicolaus *Copernicus* or his theories, esp. his heliocentric model of the universe; [adj.]

Copper Age, the or **the Chalcolithic** an archaeological period that incl. human manipulation of copper – first of the three *Metal Ages*, before *bronze* and *iron*; [Ancient Greek *khalkós* copper + *líthos* stone]

coquecigrue a chimera; a fabled creature with a lion's head, a goat's body, and a dragon's tail; [French]

Cornelian cherry a type of fruit similar to cherry; the tree that bears *Cornelian cherries* – native to parts of Europe and SW Asia; [noun]

cornigerous horned; having horns; [adj.]; [dated & rare]; "*cornigerous* fauna"

Cosa Nostra the Sicilian mafia; [proper noun]; [Italian & Sicilian, literally: *our thing*]

cosmocentric focused on the universe or cosmos; [very rare adj.]; [noun: *cosmocentrism*]; "*cosmocentric* philosophies"

cosmological horizon or **cosmic light horizon** the distance from Earth beyond which it is impossible to see because light has not had enough time to travel that far since the beginning of the universe; [noun]

cosseted pampered; [adj.]; [synonym: *coddled*]

cotquean or **cot-quean** a man who engages in tasks traditionally within a woman's purview; a female cuckold; a cuckquean; [obsolete]; [first definition synonym: *nestcock*]; [Hindi *khāṭ* (cot, bedstead)]

countercharm something working against a charm or spell; [noun]; [synonym: *counterspell*]

countercoup a sudden overthrow (initiated by a relatively small group of people) of a government that was recently so overthrown; [noun]

counterglow a subtle brightening of the night sky directly opposite the sun; [synonym: *gegenschein*]

counterspy a spy working in counterespionage; to engage in counterespionage; [noun & verb]

courtcraft the charm, negotiation skills, deceptions, and plottings used to further one's interests in a royal court; the skills needed for success in racquet sports, esp. tennis; [noun]; "Born neither handsome nor rich, the duke still, to his credit, managed to excel in *courtcraft*."

cragsman (pl. *cragsmen*) a male rock climber, esp. if skilled or accomplished; [feminine: *cragswoman*]

crash collective term for a group of rhinos; [noun]; "The angry *crash of rhinos* killed two men and obliterated their bushcamp."

cream crackered tired; exhausted; knackered; [adj.]; [Cockney rhyming slang]; "I can't pub it tonight mate – this week left me *cream crackered*!"

creedsman (pl. *creedsmen*) a fervent male follower of a particular set of religious beliefs or doctrine

croftland good quality land, upon which crops may be raised; [Scotland]

crowdsensing the compilation of measurements of a given phenomenon from dispersed individuals; "the *crowdsensing* of trail use data"

crust punk or **stenchcore** a musical genre often with dark lyrics that explore social ills – evolved in the early 80s in England

Cryogenian a geologic period from 720-635 million years BCE; during this period the *Sturtian Glaciation* froze the Earth into *Snowball Earth* for 70 million years; [Ancient Greek *krýos* (cold) + *génesis* (source, birth)]

cryogenic liquid a liquid (often a liquified gas) with a very low boiling point; [noun]; "Liquid helium, the king (or ice-queen?) of all known *cryogenic liquids*, boils at -452 Fahrenheit – only 7.5 degrees above absolute zero!"

cryosphere all areas of Earth, at any given time, where water is in a solid form such as ice or snow;

[adj. *cryospheric*]; "The affluent European alpinist may lament glacial evanescence as a cruel aspect of the Holocene's *cryospheric* diminishment – but does he consider the thirsty South Asian, for whom rapidly melting Himalayan glaciers may be a matter of life or death?"

crystalline like crystals; bright and see-through; composed of crystals; pure; [adj.]; "The sky was a deep, *crystalline* blue, and the stars were few and faint." – Willa Cather, *The Bohemian Girl*, 1912

cryptomnesia a memory bias wherein something remembered is perceived as a new and original inspiration, rather than just a memory; [noun]; [example: *a poet crafting a line of verse without realizing it is from a published poem*]

cupidity an inordinate desire for wealth or power; very greedy; strongly desiring more of something than one needs, esp. money; [synonym: *avarice*]; "I have tried... to enlist the co-operation of other capitalists, but experience has taught me that any appeal is futile that does not impinge directly upon *cupidity*."
– Robert Barr, *Lord Stranleigh Abroad*, 1913

cyclonic of or like a cyclone; characterized by fierce winds; [adj.]; "Tied one set apiece with a 5-4 game lead, the *cyclonic* topspin of her matchpoint backhand smash is inarguably the finest, most sublime of Wimbledon moments."

cynanthropy the belief that one is a dog or in the form of a dog; the ability to change into a dog and back again; [noun]; [Ancient Greek *kunikós* dog-like]

Czech lands or **Bohemian lands** the three historical regions of *Bohemia*, *Moravia*, and *Czech Silesia* that now collectively form the Czech Republic, AKA *Czechia*; [historical]

D

dactyloscopy the forensic analysis of fingerprints as a way to identify people; [noun]; [adj. *dactyloscopic*]; [Ancient Greek *dáktulos* (finger) + *skopéō* (I look at)]

daedalist a pilot; anyone who flies; [very rare noun]; [in Greek myth., *Daedalus* made wings to escape Crete with his son Icarus, but Icarus doomed himself by flying too close to the Sun and melting the wax in his wings]

Dalecarlian runes or **dalrunes** a runic script still used by some in the Swedish province of *Dalarna* into the 20th century

dalesman (pl. *dalesmen*) a person from *Yorkshire Dales* or the *Lake District* in England; [feminine: *daleswoman*]

Daliesque akin to Salvador *Dalí*, esp. to his surreal artistic style; [adj.]; "*Daliesque* dreams"

dank meme a purposefully zany meme, often featuring oversaturated colors, crude humor, or obnoxious sounds; an ironic or offensive meme, esp. if overused; a meme popular with a fringe or objectionable subgroup of the population; [rare noun]; [Internet slang]

Dark Doodad Nebula a nebula that can be viewed with binoculars as a dark arc three degrees long in the southern constellation *Musca* (the fly)

Dark Romanticism a literary and artistic subgenre of *Romanticism* emphasizing irrational, grotesque, demonic, and self-destructive themes, *et alia*; exponents incl. writers Edgar Allen Poe, Lord Byron, Herman Melville and artists Johann Fuseli, William Blake, and Francisco Goya

dark triad, **the** a psychological theory describing three offensive, but non-pathological, personality traits that may overlap within an individual: *Machiavellianism* (amoral, self-interested manipulation), *narcissism* (grandiose egotism without empathy), and *psychopathy* (selfish and callous antisocial behavior)

darkener someone or something that causes darkness or that bedims; [noun]; "Absinthe, that slow *darkener* of artistic souls..."

darkling in darkness or obscurity; dark; getting dark; darkening; [adverb & adj.]; [poetic];
"Ah, love, let us be true
To one another! for the world, which seems
To lie before us like a land of dreams,
So various, so beautiful, so new,
Hath really neither joy, nor love, nor light...
And we are here as on a *darkling* plain
Swept with confused alarms of struggle and flight,
Where ignorant armies clash by night."
– Matthew Arnold, *Dover Beach*, 1867

dark-winged blood bee a blood bee endemic to North Africa and most of Eurasia; the females are *cleptoparasitic*, entering nests of larger bees, consuming a host egg, and then laying their own

Darwin Mounds hundreds of undersea sand mounds covering 100 square kilometers about 100 miles NW of Scotland and 1000 meters below the North Atlantic Ocean – unique globally for their roughly teardrop shape; [named after a research vessel, which was named after evolutionary theorist Charles *Darwin*]

dastardize to make cowardly; to intimidate; [dated verb]; "*dastardize* my courage" – Dryden

dauntless not subject to fear or intimidation; intrepid; fearless; [adj.]; [synonym: *daredevil*]; [Latin *domitō* (I tame)]; "a *dauntless* hero"

dead cat strategy or **deadcatting** a political strategy wherein a person (esp. a politician or staff) makes a shocking announcement to divert attention (esp. media attention) away from a damaging or highly fraught subject; [based on the notion that tossing a *dead cat* on the dining room table will immediately serve to change the subject of the conversation]

decadescent decaying; [adj.]; "Pale and yellowing leaves; lives autumnal and *decadescent*."

decorous polite; formal; proper; [adj.]; [antonym: *indecorous*]; "But who can fathom the subtleties of the human heart? Certainly not those who expect from it only *decorous* sentiments and normal emotions." – Somerset Maugham, 1919

demesne a lord's manor house and grounds; a region; a domain; [noun];
"Oft of one wide expanse had I been told
That deep-brow'd Homer ruled as his *demesne*;"
– John Keats, *On First Looking into Chapman's Homer*, 1816

Demogorgon a pagan demon associated with the underworld – a powerful primordial being; [Ancient Greek *gorgós* (grim, terrible)]

demonifuge a method to expunge or protect against demons; [very rare noun]

Denisovian an extinct species of *archaic human* that spread across Asia during the Paleolithic age; Denisovians interbred with modern humans and Neanderthals; [*Denisova* Cave in the Altai Mountains of Siberia]

de-roofing or **deroofing** to remove part of the outer layer of a cyst to aid in the healing process; [Old English *hróf* (ceiling, roof, heaven, sky)]

desacralized divested of sacred aspects; stripped of holy, religious, or spiritual qualities

descamisado a term sometimes applied to Spanish revolutionaries or to followers of Juan Perón in Argentina; [Spanish *descamisado* shirtless]

descry to catch sight of, esp. from afar; to discover through eyesight; [literary verb]; "Dimly through the mists they could *descry* the long arm of the mountains rising on their left."
– J. R. R. Tolkien, *The Two Towers*, 1954

desire line, **desire path**, or **bootleg trail** an unplanned, direct short trail created when humans or animals depart from the established path, often degrading vegetation and compacting soils in the alternative track

desquamate to peel off in scales; [verb]; [noun: *desquamation*]; [Italian *squama* scale]; "Sadly, he watched the sandspout *desquamate* the clay-tiled roofs of the dwellings in the valley below."

detritus (pl. *detrita*) pieces of rock from erosion; waste material from decomposing plants and animals; any debris or fragments; [adj. *detrital* or *detritic*]; [Latin *dētero* (rub away)]; "The forest floor was moist and *detrital*."

deucedly extremely; quite; [adverb]; [synonym: *awfully*]; "*deucedly* difficult"

deus ex machina a very unlikely resolution to a story that does not honor the story's internal logic; a contrived solution to a problem, relying on some external agency; [noun]; [Latin, literally: *god from a machine*]; [in ancient Greek and Roman drama, *machinery* was often used to bring a *god* onto stage];
"He appeared like a bolt from the blue, or a *deus ex machina*, to save the day."

deuteranopes the group of human males (estimated to be 10% of the population) who lack the green retinal receptor

devaraja in medieval SE Asia, a religious order led by a god-king; [Sanskrit *deva* (exalted, divine being) + *raja* (king)]

dewbeam a beam of light, esp. sunlight, reflected off of dew; [noun]; "*Dewbeams* still glimmered in the meadow below as he woke to a morning bright and warm."

dilucular of, relating to, or occurring during dawn or the early morning; [adj.]; "*dilucular* wanderings"; [antonyms: *vespertine* & *crepuscular*]

dimmity dusk; twilight; [noun]; [synonyms: *twitterlight, cockshut* & *blue hour*]

disconsolate gloomy; dreary; inconsolable; [adj.]; [synonym: *downcast*]; "He usually kept his spirits up, but there were *disconsolate* dungeon days."

disembowered deprived of, or removed from, a bower – a shady & leafy recess in a rural garden or a wooded area; "Streams numberless, that many a fountain feeds, / Shine, *disembowered*, and give rise to sun & breeze."
– William Cullen Bryant, *The Ages*, 1821

Disneyesque or **Disneyish** similar to or reminiscent of the style of animator Walt Disney or Disney amusement parks; [adj.]; "*Disneyesque* fantasies"

displuviate in some way protected from rainfall; [very rare adj.]; [English, French, and Spanish *pluvial* (relating to rain)]; "*displuviate* coverings"

disporting amusing oneself by frolicking or moving about playfully; the action of someone who disports; [verb & noun]; [synonym: *gamboling*]; "I must fain resign all poetic *disportings* of the fancy, and pursue my narrative in humble prose."
– Washington Irving, *A History of New York*, 1809

disprivacied stripped of privacy; lacking privacy; [adj.]; [poetic & very rare]; [Latin *prīva* (one each, private)]; "Youth suffers little the third-world indignity of *disprivacied* sleeping arrangements."

diversivolent desiring a diverse array of various things; [very rare adj.]; [French *vouloir* (to want)]

divine proportion or **golden ratio** two quantities are in *golden ratio* if $(a + b) / a = a / b$; this ratio is present in some patterns in nature (e.g. the spiral arrangement of leaves) and has inspired the work of artists, architects, musicians, biologists, *et alia*; [mathematics & geometry]

dolce far niente indulgent and blissful relaxation or idleness; the enjoyment of being idle; [noun]; [Italian *dolce far niente* (sweet idleness)]; "The *dolce far niente* of that summer afternoon proved sanative to mind and body."

Dolly Daydream a woman that daydreams often; a woman with her head in the clouds; [rare]

dolorous filled with a solemn or heavy sadness; sorrowful; dismal; [adj.]; "A sable wraith she was in the parkland, fading away into the *dolorous* crypt of winter." – Michael Arlen, *Piracy: A Romantic Chronicle of These Days*, 1922

Doon Edin the Manx name for Edinburgh, Scotland

Drachenkampf or **Chaoskampf** a common motif in mythologies around the world that features a culture hero or a god fighting a *chaos monster*, often in the form of a dragon or serpent; [German, literally: *struggle against chaos*]

dragonesque dragon-like; resembling a dragon; [adj.]; "While not actually being combustive, I still considered it fair to describe her breath as *dragonesque*."

Dravidian a group of related ethnicities in southern Asia, esp. India; any one of the languages of these aboriginal groups; any member of these groups; relating to any Dravidian people or their language; [noun & adj.]; "*Dravidian* languages"

dream trance or **dream house** a subgenre of trance music (electronic dance music) – its popularity on the international dance scene peaked in the late 1990s

dreambound deep asleep and dreaming; [adj.]; [poetic & rare]; "Hers was a summer of long, active days and short, *dreambound* nights."

dreameries places particularly suitable for dreaming; [rare noun]; "That golden hour light peopled the countryside with the *dreameries* of fairyland: from shady bower, to twilit meadow & mysteried ruin."

dreamwrapt fully absorbed in dreams; preoccupied with one's thoughts or daydreams; [poetic & rare]; "...stand on a hill at a small hour of the night, and, having first expanded with a sense of difference from the mass of civilized mankind, who are *dreamwrapt* and disregardful of all such proceedings at this time, long and quietly watch your stately progress through the stars."
– T. Hardy, *Far from the Madding Crowd*, 1874

Driftless Area an American topographical & cultural region that was never covered by ice during the last Ice Age – incl. SW Wisconsin, SE Minnesota, NE Iowa, and part of NW Illinois

drogulus (pl. *droguli*) something (such as a disembodied being) that exists, but cannot be verified because it is completely intangible; [very rare noun]; [coined by 20th c. English philosopher A. J. Ayer]

dune slack the trough or valley between sand dunes; [noun]; [Gaulish *dunum* hill]

dunesand loose sand easily transported by the wind

dungeon synth a subgenre of electronic music merging the subgenres *black metal* and *dark ambient* – often paired with medieval and fantasy motifs; [noun]

Dunning-Kruger effect a pattern of deviation from normal rationality wherein persons with low ability or knowledge of a type of task or area of expertise tend to overestimate their capacities; [example: *a much higher percentage of people think they could safely land an airplane than the percentage that actually could*]

dust on crust ideal skiing conditions for some, when just a few inches of light snow has recently fallen upon a crustal layer that fully supports the skier

dustmote a single speck of dust; [noun]; [Old English *mot* (grain of sand, atom)]

Dutch tilt or **Dutch angle** in cinematography, an angled camera shot used to portray psychological tension and heavily associated with *German expressionist cinema*; [*Dutch* here is not related to the Netherlands, but a bastardization of *Deutsch* (German)]

dwale a delusion; to mutter delusively; a sleep-inducing drink or potion; [noun & verb]; [last meaning archaic]; [Afrikaans *dwaal* (a dreamy, dazed, bewildered state)]

dysphoriant something that creates an unhappy or unwell feeling or state of being; [noun]; [antonym: *euphoriant*]; "*dysphoriant* rains"

Dzungarian Gate or **Altai Gap** a mountain pass between Kazakhstan and China – the only gap in the mountains that stretch for roughly 3000 miles between Manchuria and Afghanistan

E

echelon a level or rank differentiating persons in a profession, society at large, or any organization;

in cycling, when riders maximize drafting
efficiency in a crosswind by riding in a diagonal
line; [noun]; [Spanish *escalera* (stairs, ladder)]

echinate prickly; bristled; [adj.]; [Latin *echināta*
prickly]; "*echinate* shrubbery"

echoic echo-like; of or relating to an echo;
in imitation of a natural sound; [adj.];
[synonym: *onomatopoeic*]; [antonym: *anechoic*];
"Their *echoic* vocalizations sounded nothing like
the birds they were trying to mimic."

Eddington luminosity or **Eddington limit** a star's
maximum possible luminosity when in *hydrostatic
equilibrium* – that is, when the force acting
outward (radiation) is balanced with the force
acting inward (gravitation); [Sir Arthur *Eddington*,
20th c. English astronomer]

edentulous missing teeth that are normally present;
toothless; [adj.]; [synonym: *edentate*]; [antonym:
dentulous]; [Asturian & Spanish *diente* tooth]

edgelands the transitional zone between urban and
rural areas that usually contains natural spaces
alongside often unsightly but necessary
infrastructure such as power stations; [noun]

efferent carrying outward or away from; [adj.];
[antonym: *afferent*]; [often used in biology];
"*efferent* pathways"

effrenate unrestrained or unbridled, esp. describing
passions; [obsolete adj.]; [Italian & Spanish
freno (brake, restraint)]

effulgent or **affulgent** radiant; shining; [adj.];
[noun: *effulgence*]; [Portuguese *fuligem* soot]

Egg of Columbus a seemingly creative or brilliant
idea or discovery that appears simple or obvious

after the fact; [an apochryphal story relates that after being told a new trade route was no great accomplishment, Columbus challenged his critics to stand an egg on end – they soon gave up, and Columbus flattened the egg's end by tapping it on the table]

eiderdown or **eider down** the down of an eider duck, which is often used to stuff pillows or quilts; a quilt so stuffed; "A great sea lifted us high and, crashing down with a deafening roar, carried us swiftly along on light foam as soft as *eiderdown*." – Robert D. Frisbee, *The Book of Puka-Puka*, 1929

Eight Auspicious Signs or **Ashtamangala** eight symbols that serve as helpful tools toward enlightenment; they are: the conch; endless knot; pair of golden fish; lotus; parasol; vase; wheel of dharma; and the victory banner; [Buddhism]

élan vital any mysterious or creative vital force, esp. of life itself; [noun]; [coined in 1907 by French philosopher Henri Bergson]; "We prefer Freud's Sex to Jung's Libido or Bergson's *Elan Vital*." –D.H. Lawrence, *Fantasia of the Unconscious*, 1922

eldritch eerie; supernatural; [adj.]; [possibly Old English *el-* (strange, other) + *rīce* (realm)]; "*eldritch* cackles"

elephantry military term for troops mounted on war elephants; "Sometimes Hannibal is celebrated for his creative use of *elephantry* – yet few elephants survived the Alps, and did plying them with wine before battle really help?"

elfland or **elfenland** a land peopled by elves; the homeland of elves; [noun]; "O, sweet and far from cliff and scar

The horns of *Elfland* faintly blowing!"
– Alfred, Lord Tennyson, *The Splendor Falls*, 1850

elite projection the belief among relatively affluent and influential people that what they think is convenient or attractive is good for the rest of society too; [noun]

elixir in alchemy, a liquid that changes lead to gold, cures all ills, or grants eternal life; a panacea; [noun]; [Turkish *iksir* (elixir, potion)]

elusory describing something that eludes; evasive; [adj.]; [synonym: *elusive*]

embarrassment collective term for a group of giant pandas

embowered to be surrounded as if in a leafy recess of a garden or wood; "Clusters of villages, *embowered* in luxuriant foliage, and crimson with flowers, fringed the lake." – John Abbott, *Hernando Cortez, Makers of History*, 2010

emendation the act of altering and improving something or correcting something erroneous, esp. when editing a text; [noun]; "He deemed his editor's *emendations* excellent, on the whole."

éminence grise a secret decision-maker or person of powerful inflence, esp. influence on a monarch or high official; [from a 17th c. French friar who wore a grey habit and was a confidant of Cardinal Richelieu, whose honorific was *Eminence*]; [French, literally: *grey eminence*]

Emma's giant rat or **Emma's uromys** a species of rodent only known to exist, in dwindling numbers, on the very small Indonesian island of *Owi*

emmarble or **enmarble** to change into marble; to harden; [verb]; [poetic & very rare]

emmew to mew; to confine, esp. in a coop or cage; [obsolete verb]

emotional geography an interdisciplinary field focusing on how human emotions relate to and affect the surrounding environment, including how emotions influence one's perception of a particular place

empierce to pierce; to penetrate; [rare verb]; "The lance *empierced* his armor as if only leather."

empire blue a medium blue color; [noun]

emplume to furnish with, or as with, a plume of feathers; [rare verb]

Empousa a being with one leg of copper and the ability to appear as various beasts as well as a human female; [Greek myth.]

Encantado a river dolphin known for musical talents and seduction – loves parties and may take human form by night but must wear a hat to hide its blowhole, which does not disappear after shapeshifting; [South American myth.]; [Portuguese *encantado* enchanted]

enchorial indigenous; native; [adj.]; [synonym: *autochthonous*]; [Ancient Greek *enkhórios* (of the country)]; "*enchorial* ruins"

encipher to encrypt; [verb]; [antonym: *decipher*]; [Arabic *ṣafara* (to be empty)]; "*enciphered* messages"

enforest to turn to forest; [verb]

enigmatology the scientific study of puzzles; [Greek *aínigma* puzzle]

enkindle to arouse or inspire; to kindle; "Her
   enkindling wit many sublime feelings elicited."

enlacement the state of being surrounded with
   lace, or as if with lace; "Her throat was contracted,
   her breasts strove against the *enlacement* of her
   stays, she was about to weep."
   – Norman Lindsay, *Redheap*, 1930

enravish to enrapture; to fill with delight;
   to fascinate; [verb]; [noun: *enravishment*]

enripen to ripen; to bring to perfection;
   [archaic verb]

enrobed adorned with a robe; covered as if with a
   robe; [verb]; [noun: *enrobement*];
   "Wherefore, brother, art thou weeping,
   Merry birch *enrobed* in silver,
   Silver-leaved and silver-tasselled?"
   – Elias Lönnrot, *Kalevala* (a Finnish epic), 1835

enshaded cast in shade or kept in darkness; having
   different shades; [adj.]; [archaic & poetic];
   "O soft embalmer of the still midnight,
   Shutting, with careful fingers and benign,
   Our gloom-pleas'd eyes, embower'd from the light,
   Enshaded in forgetfulness divine:"
   – John Keats, *To Sleep*, 1820

ensky to set in the sky; to elevate or exalt; [verb];
   "I failed against the affluent tide;
   Out of this abject earth of me
   I was translated and *enskied*
   Into the heavenly-regioned She."
   – Francis Thompson, *Grace of the Way*, late 19th c.

epershand ampersand; the & symbol; [Scotland];
   [Latin *et* (and) + *per se* (by itself) + English *and*]

epic simile or **Homeric simile** a detailed and lengthy direct comparison in the form of a simile; [from the lengthy *similes* employed by *Homer* in both his *epics*]; "It's crackling roots blazed and hissed – as a blacksmith plunges a glowing ax or adze in an ice-cold bath and the metal screeches steam and its temper hardens – that's the iron's strength – so the eye of Cyclops sizzled round that stake." – Homer, *The Odyssey*

epichoric of or relating to a specific location; local; [rare adj.]; [Greek *chóra* (country, homeland)]

epigone (eh-PUH-goan) a follower or disciple; any inferior imitator, esp. of a famous artist; someone less talented than his or her ancestors; [noun]; [adj. *epigonic*]; [Ancient Greek *gónos* (fruit, seed)]; "*epigonic* art"

epiphany an often awe-inspiring realization or discovery; the appearance of a divine being; [noun]; [adj. *epiphanic*]; [first def. synonym: *aha moment*]; [Ancient Greek *epí* (upon) + *phaínō* (I reveal, I shine)]

epithelium or **epithelial tissue** (pl. *epithelia*) one of the four basic types of animal tissue (others are the muscle, connective, and nervous tissues) comprised of a thin protective layer of cells; [noun]; [example: *human skin*]

epithymetic pertaining to desire or appetite; [adj.]; [dated & rare]; [Ancient Greek *epí* (on, at) + *thūmós* (soul, heart)]

epochal relating to an epoch; monumental; extremely important; [adj.]; "*epochal* events"

epyllion (pl. *epyllia*) a shortish epic poem; a short narrative poem, usually with a romantic or mythological theme; [Dutch *epyllium* epyllion]; [Ancient Greek *épos* (something spoken)]

equanimous calm and collected; mentally balanced and stable; [archaic adj.]; [synonym: *composed*]; [Latin *aequa* equal + *animus* mind]

equivorous horse-eating; [Latin *equus* (horse) + *vorare* (to eat greedily)]; [adj.]; "When the horse expired, the men quickly made a fire and did eat so greedily of the roasted (though still ghastly) flesh that the captain wondered how fine were the lines between *equivorous* and cannibalistic."

Erewhonian relating to or akin to the fictional utopia of *Erewhon*, esp. fearing machines will take over; [rare adj.]; [from Samuel Butler's 1892 novel *Erewhon* – nearly the reverse spelling of *nowhere*]

erotomania a disorder wherein one has the delusion of being in a relationship with someone; excessive sexual desire; [other nouns: *erotomaniac & erotomane*]

erstwhile former; previous; [literary adj.]; [synonyms: *onetime & quondam*]; [English *erst* (first, formerly) + *while*]; "her *erstwhile* paramour"

Escherian or **Escheresque** resembling or akin to the works of 20th c. Dutch artist M. C. *Escher*; having an impossible geometry; [rare adj.]; "The directions given seemed *Escherian*, and he soon became lost."

especial exceptional; special; particular; [adj.]; "her *especial* talents"

esquamulose in botany & mycology, having no scales; not scaly; scaleless; [antonym: *squamose*]; [Italian *squama* (fish or reptile scale)]

estrapade the actions of a horse trying to dislodge its rider; [noun]; [French]

estrie a beautiful female vampire able to fly if its hair is unbound and able to appear as human or animal; [Jewish folklore]; [French *strix* (night owl)]

Estuary English an English accent associated with London and areas along the River Thames and its *estuary* – falls somewhere between *Cockney* and *Received Pronunciation* (traditionally, the most prestigious accent);
"She spoke *Estuary English* & Peninsular Spanish, and he but several obscure Panslavonian tongues – yet wordless lovers share a language clear..."

esurient extremely hungry; ravenous; eager; [adj.]; [archaic & humorous]; [Latin]

et alia a Latin term meaning *and others* and often abbreviated *et al.* at the end of lists of people or things; [In this volume, *et alia* is never shortened and its other (strictly correct, but cumbersome) Latin grammatical cases are ignored.]

et in Arcadia ego an inscription on tombs in two classical 17th c. paintings (one Italian, one French); meant as a warning that death is present even in paradise; [rare phrase]; [Latin, literally: *I too was in Arcadia*]

etesian winds or **meltemi** strong and dry north winds of the Aegean Sea – most active in late spring and summer; [Turkish *meltem* (sea breeze)]

ethereal darkwave a subgenre of darkwave music influenced by Gothic rock and developed in the early 80s in the UK – prominently represented by the bands *Cocteau Twins* and *This Mortal Coil*

etherize to transform into ether; to render insensible or unconscious by inhalation of ether; [verb]; [obsolete adj. *ethereous*]; "When the evening is spread out against the sky Like a patient *etherized* upon a table" – T. S. Eliot, *The Love Song of J. Alfred Prufrock*, 1917

ethren plural of *other*; [archaic & very rare]

eudemonia or **eudaimonia** general happiness; a state of prosperity and health; [rare noun]; [adj. *eudemonic*]; [Ancient Greek *eu-* (good) + *daímōn* (goddess, spirit)]

eumorphous having a pleasing shape; well-formed; [very rare adj.]; [Greek *morfí* (form, shape)]

euphonious (you-FOH-nee-us) sounding pleasant; having *euphony*; pleasing to the ear, esp. such speech; [adj.]; "*euphonious* voices"

Eurasian blue tit a small perching bird of blue and yellow plumage indigenous to European subarctic deciduous forests and feeding upon insects & spiders

eutrapelia or **eutrapely** the art of conversation and wit; [very rare noun]; [Ancient Greek]

evanescent disappearing; vanishing; ephemeral; fleeting; [adj.]; [noun: *evanescence*]; [antonym: *nonevanescent*];
"The sea was each little bird's great playmate... In their airy flutterings, they seemed to rest on the *evanescent* spray." – Nathaniel Hawthorne, *Footprints on the Sea-shore*, 1842

evenfall twilight; dusk; [poetic noun]; [synonyms: *cockshut*, *crepusculum*, *twitterlight*, and *mirkning*]; "The wind that blows across them calls
Ever at dawns and *evenfalls*,
And I am suddenly forlorn.
Across the pastures and ripe corn
I see the mountains in my dreams."
– Katharine Tynan, *The Exile*, 1905

excrementitious like excrement; consisting of matter proper to be evacuated from the body; [adj.]; "I absolve you from all except yourself, spiritual, bodily – that is eternal, / (The corpse you will leave will be but *excrementitious*.)"
– Walt Whitman, *Leaves of Grass*, 1860

excrescence something growing out of another thing, esp. if abnormal; [noun]; [adj. *excrescent*]

excretive having the power of excreting; promoting excretion; [adj.]; [synonym: *excretory*]; "Black coffee – the most *excretive* of drugs."

exemplar something or someone deserving of imitation; a role model; [noun]

exemplum (pl. *exempla*) an example; a parable; a story that communicates a moral principle

exfiltrate to stealthily withdraw, esp. troops or other military personnel, from a perilous situation; [verb]; [antonym: *infiltrate*]

exosphere the outermost layer of a planet's atmosphere; [noun]

extragalactic astronomy the scientific study of objects outside the Milky Way galaxy

extrality immunity, esp. if diplomatic, from the local laws of a certain geographic area; [shortening of *extraterritoriality*]; "The *extrality* inherent to her embassy position seemed to shorten the interval twixt arrest & release – the others were detained overnight."

extremophile an organism that survives, or even thrives, under extreme environmental conditions, such as high heat, acidity, air pressure, etc.; [noun]; [adj. *extremophilic*]

extrospection the perception (or reasoning consideration) of things external to one's own mind; [noun]; [antonym: *introspection*]

F

fadelessly without fading; eternally; [poetic adj.]

fairylore the study or history of fairies; [noun]

falciform shaped like a sickle; [adj.]; [Italian *falce* (scythe; sickle)]; "What announced the accomplishment of this rise in temperature? A double *falciform* ejection of water vapour from under the kettlelid at both sides simlutaneously." – James Joyce, *Ulysses*, 1922

false map turtle an American turtle species that loves to bask in the sun

fantasque fantastical; [obsolete adj.]; [French]

fantod or **fantad** an extreme feeling of nervous anxiety; irritability; [noun]; [possibly from English *fantastic* + Welsh *-od* (plural ending)]

Fata Morgana Land a phantom island first sighted off the NE coast of Greenland in 1907; [*Fata Morgana*, a type of mirage caused by light bending due to temperature differentials]

fatiloquent prophetic; speaking of fate or destiny; [dated adj.]; [synonym: *fatidical*]; [Latin *fatum* fate + *loqui* speak]; "*fatiloquent* seers"

favillous like ashes; consisting of ashes; [obsolete adj.]; [Italian *favilla* (spark, glimmer)]

feliform resembling a cat (or any member of the suborder Feliformia) in appearance; [adj.]; [Latin *fēlis* cat]

felinity the condition of being a cat; collective term for all cats; any characteristic common in felines; "The pampered life of American *felinity*."

fellifluous flowing with gall; audacious; impudent; [rare adj.]; [Latin *fel* (gall, poison)]

Felliniesque surreal; similar to or reminiscent of the style of Italian film director Federico *Fellini*; [adj.]; "*Felliniesque* parties, elaborate and strange."

felonious malicious; traitorous; perfidious; having the nature of a crime; done with the deliberate purpose to commit a crime; [adj.];
"O thievish Night,
Why should'st thou, but for some *felonious* end,
In thy dark lantern thus close up the stars?"
– John Milton, *Comus*, 1637

Fermi paradox the paradox of there being no solid evidence of advanced extraterrestrial life even though it's highly probable that a great many instances of such life exist; [Enrico *Fermi*, Italian-American physicist (1901-1954)]

fernland a land of many ferns; [rare noun]; "Frolicking free through field, forest & *fernland*..."

fervescent growing hot; [adj.]; [Spanish *hervir* (to boil, to seeth)]

feuillemorte (few-oolay-mort) the color of a faded leaf; yellowish-brown; [adj.]; [French *feuille* leaf + *morte* dead]; "The *feuillemorte* forests of autumn"

Finnsburg Fragment the 50-line surviving fragment of an Old English heroic poem – features a Prince defending *Finn's fort*; [noun]

firebolt a missile of fire; to strike with a firebolt; [noun & verb]; "For days the besiegers launched *firebolts* over the castle walls."

fire cloud or **pyrocumulus cloud** a dense cumuliform cloud formed from a large fire or a volcanic eruption; [noun]

fire philosopher an alchemist; [obsolete]; "Twas not for love of wine, that Jesus turned the waters; So too do *fire philosophers* aurify not to sate a gilded lust."

fireflied lit up by little points of light; [poetic adj.]; "the *fireflied* skies of a southern night"

five children of Iblis, **the** five devils (Dasim, Awar, Sut, Theber, and Zalanpur), each assigned a specific type of evil task against humanity – they lay eggs to reproduce; [Islam]

five classical senses the five traditionally recognized human senses: *hearing*, *sight*, *taste*, *smell*, and *touch* – in fact humans have many more senses, including the senses of *balance*, *spatial orientation*, and *body position*

Five Eyes the alliance of the intelligence agencies of Canada, US, UK, New Zealand, and Australia, esp. regarding *signals intelligence* – one of the most fully-realized espionage alliances in world history

Five Glens of Angus the five Highland glens located in the *Angus* region of Scotland

flamberge a type of European greatsword with a wavy blade; [synonym: *flame-bladed sword*]; [French]

flamboyance collective term for a stand of
    flamingos; [rare usage]
fleece to cheat someone by overcharging; [verb];
    [UK & American slang]; "Refusing to haggle, he
    was easily and often *fleeced*."
flexion the act of bending, esp. the bending
    of a joint; deviation from a straight direction;
    a turning; [noun]; [Italian *flessione* (bend,
    inflexion)]
fluctiferous tending to create waves; [rare adj.]
fluctisonous sounding like waves; [very rare adj.]
flybridge or **flying bridge** an open area atop or
    adjacent to the pilothouse used as an operating
    station by officers during fair weather or near
    port; [noun]; [nautical]; [synonym: *monkey island*];
    "We passed them on our way to the monkey
    island, or *flying bridge*, where we could enjoy the
    best view."
    – George Fetherling, *Running Away to Sea*, 2008
Flying Foam Massacre a massacre of Aboriginal
    people by colonial settlers in 1868 in western
    Australia near Flying Foam Passage; [historical]
flyspeck housefly excrement; any very insignificant
    thing; to spray with tiny bits of color; to inspect
    with careful detail; to nitpick; [noun & verb];
    [adj. *flyspecked*]
folie à deux (pl. *folies à deux*) a rare syndrome in
    which a delusional belief is transmitted from one
    person to another – usually occurs between
    people cohabitating in isolation;
    [French *madness of two*]

folkmoot or **thing** a gathering in a town or shire to make group decisions; [the Danish parliament, the Folketing, means *the people's thing*]

fore moonsail the top sail on the foremast of a three-masted, full-rigged sailing ship

forebrain the anterior portion of the brain, incl. the *cerebrum* and both *thalami*; [synonym: *prosencephalon*]; [antonym: *hindbrain*]

foredune a dune ridge that runs parallel to a water body; "He swam to shore, crossed the beach, and hid (as best he could) among the *foredunes*."

forefeeling a premonition; a foreboding feeling; a feeling that something is going to happen, esp. something negative; [synonym: *presentiment*]; "All hope of safety, all desire of peace, All but the loathed *forefeeling* of blank death..." – James Russell Lowell, *Prometheus*, 1890

foreglimpse a revelation of the future; to catch sight of a future event; [noun & verb]; [synonym: *foregleam*]; "of *foreglimpsed* delights, she dreamt"

foreland a promontory; a headland; [noun]

forelock hair that typically covers the forehead; "Warm with the blood of lads I know Comes east the sighing air. It fanned their temples, filled their lungs, Scattered their *forelocks* free;" – A. E. Housman, *A Shropshire Lad*, 1896

foremother a female ancestor; [synonym: *ancestress*]

forename first name; given name; any name that precedes the last name or surname; [antonym: *aftername*]; "the etched *forenames* of lovers long lost"

forespoken foretold; spoken before; predicted;
"The elders were always *forespeaking* doom..."

forest bathing spending time in a forest as a
therapeutic activity; [Japanese *shinrin-yoku*];
"She immediately headed for a large nearby
wood to decompress by *forest bathing.*"

foretaste a taste before some greater thing or event;
a sample taken beforehand, esp. in anticipation;
an experience undergone before a larger event;
to taste in advance; [noun & verb]; [synonym:
pregustation]; [antonym: *aftertaste*]; "The flat
tire was but a *foretaste* of the journey's many
challenges."

forlorn abandoned; deserted; hopeless; miserable;
lonely and sad, esp. from feeling forsaken; [adj.];
[Dutch *plompverloren* (completely lost)];
"Thou wast not born for death, immortal bird! ...
The voice I hear this passing night was heard
In ancient days ...
The same that oft-times hath
Charmed magic casements, opening on the foam
Of perilous seas in fairy lands *forlorn.*"
– Keats, *Ode to a Nightingale*, 1819

Formosa an old name for the island of Taiwan;
[adj. *Formosan*]; [Portuguese *formosa* beautiful]

Fortunate Isles, the winterless islands in the Atlantic
Ocean where Greek heroes enjoyed an afterlife of
musical and athletic pursuits; [Greek myth.]

foxtrot oscar euphemism for *f*ck off*;
[NATO phonetic alphabet]

frantling the vocalizations made by peafowl;
a peacock's mating call; [very rare noun]

fraught laden; entailing; accompanied by; equipped; causing distress, esp. through complexity; [adj.]; "The journey was *fraught* with diverse dangers."

fremdschämen (fremd-shaymen) to feel ashamed about another person's actions; [very rare verb]; [synonym: *vicarious embarrassment*]; [German *fremd* (external) + *schämen* (to be ashamed)]

frenulum a fold of tissue that supports or restrains that to which it is attached, esp. the folds of skin beneath the tongue or between lip and gums; [noun]; [anatomy]; [Latin *little bridle*]

frigorific causing cold; making cold or colder; [adj.]; [antonym: *calorific*]; "*frigorific* winds"

frisson, **aesthetic chills**, or **psychogenic shivers** a psychophysiological response to certain rewarding cultural stimuli (most often music) wherein one gets a pleasurable feeling of chills and skin tingling; frisson may also be invoked by poetry, natural beauty, inspired speeches, *et alia*, and usually lasts only a few seconds – the exciting cause of frisson is very specific to each individual; [French *frisson* shiver]

frondescence the time when a plant unfolds its leaves; the action of same; [noun]; "Every spring he anticipated the treed hillside's *frondescence*."

frostbound frozen; bound by frost; [adj.]; "*frostbound* heights"

frozen assets a term for male canine reproductive material when frozen for transport or storage for later breeding purposes; [noun]

frumious extremely angry; [adj.]; [*fuming* + *furious* – coined by Lewis Carroll in *Jabberwocky*, 1871]

fulgurate to flash with (or as if with) lightning; [verb]; [Romanian *fulger* lightning]; *"fulgurating tempests"*

funistrada a fake food item inserted into a 1974 United States Army survey on food preferences – scored above eggplant, cranberry juice, grilled bologna, *et alia*; [also fake in the same survey: *braised trake* & *buttered ermal*]

furiosant furious; [rare adj.]

futurity the future; an event in the future; [noun]; "That lost in long *futurity* expire." – Thomas Gray, *The Bard: A Pindaric Ode*, 1757

G

galactico a European football superstar; [noun]; [Spanish *galáctico* galactic]

Gallophilia or **Gallimania** love or admiration of France or the French culture, people, or language; [noun]; [synonym: *Francophilia*]; [antonym: *Gallophobia*]

galumptious or **goluptious** delightful; wonderful; magnificent; [very rare adj.]

gambados leather gaiters attached to a saddle; protective leg coverings; long gaiters; [synonym: *spatterdashes*]; [Italian & Spanish *gamba* leg]

gambol to frolic; to move in a playful manner; an instance of same; a playful antic; a frolic; [verb & noun]; [French *gambade* frolic]; "Three girls moved across the billiard-table lawn of a great manor house, circling and swarming about a common center of gravity like *gamboling* sparrows." – Neal Stephenson, *The Diamond Age*

gambrinous being drunk from drinking beer; beer-loving; [very rare adj.]; [*Gambrinus*, a legendary European folk hero celebrated for his *joie de vivre* and his love of beer – often depicted as a jovial, bearded, abdominous duke]

Gamma Velorum a quadruple star system in the constellation Vela – AKA *the Spectral Gem of Southern Skies* due to its exotic spectrum

Gandvik a dangerous sea, due to its winding shape – may refer to the Gulf of Bothnia in the Baltic Sea between Finland and Sweden; [Norse myth.]

garden of the gods a Sumerian religious conception of divine paradise and home to immortals – sometimes connected to the *cedars of Lebanon*

Gardnerian witchcraft a traditional aspect of the Wicca religion, with beliefs and practices that originated from the *New Forest coven*; [Gerald *Gardner*, 20th c. English Wiccan & author]

gates of horn and ivory a literary image used to distinguish true dreams from false – dreams that enter through *gates of horn* are true, those entering by *gates of ivory* are false; [Homer, the *Odyssey*, 7th c. BCE]; [coined based on the Greek word for *horn* being similar to *fulfill* and *ivory* being similar to *deceive*]

geloscopy divination by means of laughter; a supposed way to learn a person's character by observing their laughter; [rare noun]; [Greek *gelastós* smiling]

genius loci (pl. *genii locorum*) the minor god or goddess that watches over a certain place; figuratively, the spirit or ambience of a place, esp.

if artistically inspiring; [noun]; [synonyms: *geist* & *muse*]; [Latin *guardian deity of a place*]

geoisotherm or **isogeotherm** in geology, a line of points of equal temperature under the Earth's surface; [noun]; [adj. *isogeothermic*]

geoponics the science of cultivating the land; [Ancient Greek *pónos* (hard work)]

geostrategic pertaining to the strategy of *geopolitics* – the study of the effects of geography on international politics; geopolitically strategic; [adj.]; "Once in possession of Istanbul, the Russians would control the *geostrategic* straits of the Bosporus..."
– Eugene Rogan, *The Fall of the Ottomans*, 2015

geotectonics the study of Earth's structure, esp. with emphasis upon the *tectonic plates*; [adj. *geotectonic*]; [synonym: *tectonics*]

gerontic (jair-RON-tik) relating to old age or elderly persons; [Greek *géros* (old man)]; "*gerontic* wealth"

ghostland a region or area that is deserted like a ghost town; [noun]; "midwestern *ghostlands*"

ghostshipping the action of completely ignoring responsibilities, esp. in a relationship or a job; the act of coasting through or meeting the bare minimum requirements of a job; [rare noun]; [American slang]; [verb: *ghostship*]; "She decided to *ghostship* in protest of her demotion."

giant blind mole-rat a subterranean species of Russian rodent native to the North Caucasus

gibberbird or **desert chat** a terrestrial passerine species of bird native to Australia

gibbosity (pl. *gibbosities*) the state of being convex or protuberant; an outward bulge; [adj. *gibbous*];

"The Black Sea beach was grotesquely studded
with the bare *gibbosities* of eldern Bulgarian men."
"The night was bathed in reflected solar light –
a waxing *gibbous* nearly phased into a plenilune."

gillygaloo a bird that nests on hillsides and lays
square eggs that dont roll down the slopes;
[American folklore]

Ginnungagap the primordial void where *Niflheim's*
cold and the heat of *Muspelheim* meet in the
Norse creation myth; [Old Norse *vast void*]

girdle of Venus, the a prominent line close to the
fingers – examined in some practices of palmistry

glaciofluvial relating to water flowing within, upon,
or against glaciers; [adj.]; "*glaciofluvial* deposits"

Glasscock one of 254 counties in Texas – pop. 1100;
[George Washington *Glasscock* (1810-1868)]

Glathsheim or **Gladsheim** in Norse myth., the part
of Asgard that includes Valhalla; [Old Norse
bright home]

gleek to project saliva out of one's mouth from
under the tongue, directly from the salivary
glands; the saliva so projected; [verb & noun];
[informal]

glitterance a sparkling of light; [poetic noun];
[archaic & rare adj. *glitterant*];
"...from the *glitterance* of the sunny main,
He turn'd his aching eyes,
And then upon the beach he laid him down,
And watched the rising tide."
– Robert Southey, *Thalaba the Destroyer*, 1801

globigerina ooze fine grained sediment covering
vast areas of the ocean floor and composed

mostly of tiny shells of *Globigerina*, a genus of single-celled organisms; [noun]

glottochronology the study of languages to determine their chronological relationship, esp. when languages separated; [noun]; [Greek *glóssa* tongue]

gluteal fold the horizontal crease below each human buttock; [noun]; [anatomy]

glutinous viscous; like glue; [adj.]; "thick, *glutinous* effluvia oozed from the wound"

glutinous hag the hagfish – a primitive, eel-like fish with a sucker mouth and rasping teeth; [synonym: *slime eel*]

goblin mode a usually temporary lifestyle wherein one stops caring about one's appearance, watches TV or otherwise wastes time, doesn't go out much, and eats relatively unhealthy, often delivered food; [rare noun]; [UK slang]; "Have you seen Astrid? I heard she's in *goblin mode* again."

gobsmacked or **gobstruck** astounded; speechless; [adj.]; [synonym: *flabbergasted*]; [Irish *gob* mouth]

godhopping changing your religion for non-religious reasons, esp. to secure some benefit, to get a job, or just to follow what is fashionable

goes like a shower of sh*t impressive or fast-moving; [Australian slang]

Golden Age of Piracy, the the period from about 1650-1730 when piracy flourished in the North Atlantic and the Indian Ocean; [historical]

golden hour or **magic hour** the time period soon before sunset or after sunrise during which daylight is highly filtered through the atmosphere and therefore softer and redder – length and time of day this occurs vary due to season, latitude, topography, and atmospheric conditions; [noun]; "Of his seven poetic synonyms for twilight, she favored *golden hour* and disliked mirkning."

gonkulator a piece of equipment that may look impressive but is actually useless; any useless gadget; any mechanical device or computer hardware that is particularly loathed; [very rare]; [from the American TV series *Hogan's Heroes*]

gonopodium (pl. *gonopodia*) a modified extremity, such as a fin, of certain types of fish and anthropods used for reproduction; [noun]; [adj. *gonopodial*]

gonzo in journalism, describing a story written in an unusual, exaggerated, and very subjective manner, esp. when the reporter participates in the story's events; unconventional; bizarre; crazy; *gonzo* journalism; a wild and seemingly crazy person; [adj. & noun]; [coined by Bill Cardoso, *Boston Globe* editor, in 1970 describing Hunter S. Thompson's article *The Kentucky Derby is Decadent and Depraved*; a Muppet named Gonzo debuted later that year]

goozer a kiss; a disliked person; a lowlife; to kiss; [noun & verb]; [UK slang]; "They were seen *goozering* in a punt on the Cam."

Grand Erg Oriental a large field of sand dunes in NE Algeria – part of the Sahara Desert; [noun]

grand fromage an important person; a big shot; [informal noun]; [synonym: *grand poobah*]; [French *big cheese*]

graupel a form of precipitation that occurs when tiny water droplets freeze onto falling snowflakes;

[noun]; [synonyms: *popcorn snow* & *soft hail*];
[German *Graupen* (hulled wheat)]

graveolent having a rank odor; [rare adj.];
[noun: *graveolence*]; [Latin *gravis* heavy];
"*graveolent* stables"

Graveyard Seamounts 28 small underwater
volcanoes east of New Zealand – the largest is
named *the Graveyard* and the rest follow a
somewhat *necropolitan* naming convention,
incl. *Soul Destroyer* and *Gothic*

gravific or **gravitic** of or relating to gravity; [adj.];
[synonym: *gravitational*]; "Her attraction was
gravitic – universal, persistent, and strong."

Great African Seaforest a large, very biodiverse
forest of giant bamboo kelp off the coasts of
Namibia and South Africa

Great Dying or **Late Permian extinction event**
Earth's most severe known mass extinction event
about 250 million years BCE; 81% of marine
species, *et alia*, went extinct – possibly caused
by volcanic eruptions that flooded portions of
the Earth with basalt, and led to elevated
temperatures and ocean acidity

Great Game the 19th c. struggle between the
Russian & British Empires over influence in
Central & South Asia, esp. in Persia,
Afghanistan, and Tibet – the contest never
devolved into direct conflict between the two
empires, but was marked by diplomatic intrigue
and regional wars; [known as *the Tournament of
Shadows* in Russia]; [historical]

Great Molasses Flood a 1919 disaster in Boston's
North End in which a large storage tank burst

and released a 25-foot wave of molasses (8700 cubic meters in total) that travelled at 35 mph and killed 21 people; [historical]

Great Moon Hoax of 1835 a series of six widely-believed articles published in the New York paper *The Sun* which described life and civilization on the Moon including *Vespertilio-homo* – a bat-like species of humanoids; [historical]

Great Rift or **Dark Rift** a dark band across the night sky caused by interstellar clouds of cosmic dust that obscures one-third of the Milky Way galaxy from Earth's perspective; [astronomy]

Great Sand Sea a large sand desert (erg) within the Sahara composed mostly of sand dunes and straddling the border between Libya and Egypt

Great Stink, the an event in London in the summer of 1858 when hot weather increased the smell of human and industrial waste from a sewer system that emptied directly into the Thames; [historical]

Great Western Woodlands 40 million acres of woodlands in SW Australia – larger than England and Wales combined; includes 3500 different plant species and 138 known species of reptile

Green Spain or **the Cantabrian Coast** a lush region in northern Spain with a wet and temperate oceanic climate; [Spanish *España Verde* (Green Spain)]

green-fingered having a seeming aptitude for gardening or caring for plants; [adj.]; [UK]; [synonym: *green-thumbed*]

greenscape heavily-foliaged landscape; a mostly green area of land; [noun]; "Delightful

greenscapes unrolled out his train window
as they left the edgelands north of Glasgow."

greensward a piece of land covered in green grass;
[noun]; [adj. *greenswarded*]; "randomly-patterned
vistas of hedge, wood, and *greensward*."

gressorial in zoology, an appendage adapted for
walking rather than for another purpose; [adj.];
[Latin *gradior* (I walk)]; "*gressorial* limbs"

grey rocking pretending to be boring or
unappealing (like a plain *grey rock*) as
a strategy to avoid an annoying narcissist,
such as at a party; [verb]; [American slang]

Groom of the Stool the title of an English royal
courtier that attended to the King's toileting
needs, incl. all excretion; changed to *Groom
of the Stole* by Victorians; [Formal title:
Groom of the King's Close Stool]; [historical]

grotesquery or **grotesquerie** an unnatural or
monstrous distortion; the quality of being
gruesome and terrifying; a genre of early 20th c.
literature incorporating elements of science
fiction & horror – incl. works by Ambrose
Bierce, Fritz Leiber, and H. P. Lovecraft; [noun];
"Macabre *grotesqueries* splattered her pages,
as she penned her vivid, her lurid poetical rages."

grue any byproduct of a bloody, violent, or
gruesome event, such as gore, viscera,
blood, etc.; [noun]

grufted dirty; befouled; [rare adj.];
[synonym: *begrimed*]; "*grufted* undergear"

grundle a large amount; a bunch; the *perineum*;
[noun]; [American slang]; "a *grundle* of cousins"

H

haberdashery a shop that sells men's clothing, esp. hats; a shop selling sewing supplies; [Anglo Norman *habertas* (small goods)]

hadopelagic zone or **hadal zone** the deepest region of the ocean comprised of 46 different *hadal* habitats within the oceanic trenches – ranges from 20,000 to 36,000 feet below sea level; [*Hades* – Greek god of the underworld]

hagiography the study of saints; the biography of a saint; any very reverent or respectful biography; [adj. *hagiographic*]; [Greek *ágios* saintly]

haint blue various pale shades of blue-green – traditionally used to paint porches in the southern US; [*haint* is an alternate form of *haunt*]

halation light surrounding an object or person as if forming a halo; light forming a foggy blur around the edges of a bright area in a photo or on an old TV screen; [synonym: *overglow*]; [*halo* + -*ation*]

halitotic having *halitosis*, or foul-smelling breath; [adj.]; [Latin *hālitus* (whiff, breath)]; [Spanish *hálito* (breath, breeze, whiff)]

havenless without a refuge or place of safety; [adj.]; "in those days, we were but *havenless* runaways..."

haversack a small backpack or shoulder pack, originally made of canvas; [German *Hafer* oats]

haversine formula in *spherical trigonometry*, the formula used to calculate the great circle distance (shortest distance) between two points on a sphere given the latitude and longitude – very important historically in navigation

havoc widespread devastation; to pillage;
to leave a wide path of destruction;
[noun & verb]; [present participle: *havocking*];
[synonym: *mayhem*]

Hector the Convector a cumulonimbus thunder-
cloud cluster that forms most afternoons from
September to March over the Tiwi Islands,
Northern Territory, Australia – one of the world's
most consistently formed large thunderstorms

hellery wild or unruly behavior; [very rare noun];
"The many-pinted, midnight *hellery* of the fatbike
gang's frontman was legendary."

hemal or **hemic** relating to blood; [adj.]; [synonym:
hematic]; [Ancient Greek *haîma* blood]

hemispheric pertaining to a hemisphere; shaped
like half a sphere; [adj.]

hemistich a half line of verse set apart by a pause;
an incomplete line of verse; [noun];
[Ancient Greek *hēmi* half + *stíkhos* verse]

heptagram, **heptangle**, or **septagram** a star-shaped
symbol composed of seven straight lines; [noun];
[Romani *efta* seven]

hero snow snow with a good base for turning;
[such snow is so easy to ski or ride on that even
the less skilled feel *heroic*]

herostratic fame fame or infamy that comes from
having committed a crime or some other
misdeed; [rare noun]; [*Herostratus* was an
ancient Greek arsonist who sought fame by
setting ablaze the temple of Artemis at Ephesus
in 356 BCE]

Hesperian epoch a Martian geologic epoch
marked by lava flows – after the *Noachian* and

before the *Amazonian* about 3500 to 1800
million years BCE; [Latin *Hesperia* (western land)]

Hesperus Ski Area an alpine ski area located near
Hesperus, Colorado, America; [Ancient Greek
hésperos western]

hexapod any creature with six legs; a six-legged
robot; [noun]; [adj. *hexapodal*]; [Greek *pódi* foot]

Hibernophile one who loves the Irish people,
country, or culture; [antonym: *Hibernophobe*];
[Latin *Hibernia* Ireland]

Highveld, **the** a high plateau elevated between 1500
& 2100 meters that covers 30% of South Africa
incl. its most important agricultural areas;
[Afrikaans *Hoëveld* (high field)]

hillstream a stream running down a hillside –
typically fast-moving; [very rare noun]

hinterland a remote area, esp. if hard to access;
figuratively, anything vague or not well defined;
[German *hinter* behind + *Land* land]

hippocamp or **hippocampus** (pl. *hippocampi*)
a fantastical creature with the head and forelimbs
of a horse and hind section of a dolphin or fish;
[Roman, Greek, and other mythologies]; [Ancient
Greek *híppos* (horse) + *kámpos* (sea monster)]

historicity of Jesus the belief, shared by a vast
majority of scholars, that the person Jesus existed
historically – a separate issue from the belief in
the alleged divinity & miracles associated with
Jesus

Hoag's Object a ring galaxy in the constellation
Serpens containing roughly eight billion stars;
[discovered by Arthur *Hoag* in 1950]

Hobbesian involving competition that is entirely self-serving, unrestrained, or without civility; [adj.]; [Thomas Hobbes, 17th c. English author of *Leviathon*, 1651]; "The corporate culture was brutal – quite *Hobbesian*."

hole carding in card games (esp. *blackjack*), learning the identity of cards that are supposed to be hidden from view; types of *hole carding* incl. *first-basing* (seeing the card when the dealer checks the hole card) and *front-loading* (seeing the hole card as it is slid under the *upcard*); "He was booted for *hole carding* by rubbernecking, which the casino considers an illegal form of advantage gambling."

homosociality asexual socialization with members of the same sex; [noun]; [adj. *homosocial*]; [antonym: *heterosociality*]; "The four-day spring *homosocial* bonding ritual featured skiing, saunas, scouting, and scotch..."

honey-tongued having a pleasant voice; speaking sweetly; persuasive; [adj.]; [synonym: *silver-tongued*]; "*honey-tongued* radio personalities"

Horned Serpent a creature appearing in many Native American, as well as some European & Near Eastern, mythologies

hornswoggle to deceive; to bamboozle; [dated verb]; [American slang]

horse latitudes the area between 30 and 35 degrees both north and south latitude – characterized by clear skies, calm winds, and very limited precipitation; figuratively, a state of inactivity or torpor; [possibly from the nautical term *horsed* – when a ship rides a current in becalmed seas]

hortus conclusus a genre of garden that is enclosed and more private esp. if enclosed with an actual wall or a seemingly impenetrable and high hedge; [rare noun]; [Latin, literally: *enclosed garden*]

hotspur a person who is impulsive or who makes quick, ill-reasoned decisions in a forceful manner; [archaic noun]; [synonym: *hothead*]; [from the Shakespearean character *Hotspur* (Henry Percy) in *Henry IV, Part I*]

housecarl a household bodyguard or servant in medieval Northern Europe; [Old Norse *karl* man]

hubristic pertaining to hubris or excessive pride; very arrogant or overconfident; [rare adj.]; "Strange, not strange: how the ignorant are often the most *hubristic*."

hucklebone or **huckle bone** the hip bone; the ankle bone; [archaic noun]

humpenscrump a primitive, stringed musical instrument similar to a hurdy-gurdy; [rare noun]

hwyl (hwil) a strong emotional state or enthusiasm, esp. one that gives rise to a sudden, eloquent outburst; [rare noun]; [Welsh *hwyl* (sail, journey, fun, fervor)]

hydraulic despotism or **water monopoly empire** a governing structure that maintains power by complete control of water resources

hyperbole a deliberate or unintentional exaggeration or overstatement; [noun]; [adj. *hyperbolic*]; [antonym: *understatement*]; [Ancient Greek *hupér* (above) + *bállō* (I throw)]

hyperbolic geometry a non-Euclidean geometry that does not adhere to the *parallel postulate*

Hyperborea a bountiful land of sunshine in the far north inhabited by giants; [Greek myth.]; [Ancient Greek *hupér* above + *bóreios* northern]

Hyperion one of 12 Titans in Greek myth.; an 1819 poem by Keats; one of 146 known moons of Saturn; a genus of beetle; a coastal redwood in northern California – the world's tallest known living tree (116 meters)

hyperthymia or **hyperthymic temperament** a type of personality characterized by a very positive, upbeat, enthusiastic attitude toward life; [noun]; [adj. *hyperthymic*]; [antonym: *dysthymia*]; [Ancient Greek *hupér* excessive + *thūmós* soul]; "She was outgoing, *hyperthymic*, and generally a joy to be around – if one has the energy."

Hypnalis a legendary asp that attacked and killed people in their sleep or sometimes put them into an endless sleep; [medieval folklore]; [Greek *ýpnos* sleep]

I

Iberian ribbed newt a newt endemic to Morocco and the *Iberian* Peninsula – its sharp, poison-coated ribs can puncture its sides and act as a defense mechanism

iceberg theory or **theory of omission** the artistic belief that the deeper meaning of a narrative work of literature should not be obviously described, but rather should shine through implicitly; [espoused by Ernest Hemingway]

idée fixe (ee-day feeks) an idea that dominates the mind and that one clings to even if presented with contrary evidence; [synonym: *obsession*]; [French, literally: *fixed idea*]

idyllic very blissful, peaceful, or scenic; an *idyllic* situation; [adj. & noun]; [Ancient Greek *eîdos* (shape, beauty)]; "He could retire to the *idyllic* with the knowledge that he had not been wanting when Romance called."
– John Buchan, *Huntington Tower*, 1922

igniferous producing fire; [rare adj.]; [synonym: *flammiferous*]; [Spanish *ignífuga* fireproof]

ignifluous flowing with fire; [very rare adj.]; "... the whole area of the crater became one entire sea of *ignifluous* matter." – W. Brigham, *Volcanoes of the Hawaiian Islands*, 1840

ignimbrite a rock deposit left by a volcanic, pyroclastic flow composed mostly of ash; [noun]; [adj. *ignimbritic*]; [Latin *ignis* fire + *imbris* shower]; "*ignimbritic* deposits"

ignoble not noble; common; without honor; [noun: *ignobility*]; [Spanish *innoble* ignoble]; "Far from the madding crowd's *ignoble* strife, Their sober wishes never learn'd to stray; Along the cool sequester'd Vale of Life..."
– Thomas Gray, *Elegy Written in a Country Churchyard*, 1750

ignorati (pl. only) ignorant humans, esp. those who amplify their own ignorance by ignoring certain facts or spreading falsehoods; [rare noun]; [slang]; [synonym: *ignorami*]; [*ignorant* + *literati*]

ilinx a type of play that temporarily disrupts perception, usually by causing vertigo, disorientation, or frenzy; the changed state of consciousness that is so created; [rare noun];

[Ancient Greek *îlinx* (whirlpool, vertigo)]; [coined by 20th c. French sociologist Robert Caillois]

iliosacral pertaining to the *ilium* (a bone of the hip & pelvis) or the *sacrum* (a triangular bone at the spine's base between the two *ilia*); [adj.]; [synonym: *sacroiliac*]; [anatomy]

ilk a type, kind, or category; a group of entities that share enough characteristics to sensibly be grouped together; [noun];
"The cow is of the bovine *ilk*;
One end is moo, the other, milk."
– Ogden Nash, *The Cow*, 1931

ill-disposed not inclined toward something or someone; unsympathetic; [adj.]; "The professor was *ill-disposed* toward the unruly students."

ill-scented foul-smelling; of disagreeable odor; [adj.]; [synonym: *malodorous*]

illiterati (pl. only) a societal group of *illiterate* people; the uneducated class; the unlettered masses; [rare noun]

Illuminati historically, the Bavarian Illuminati were a secret society founded in 1776 to oppose superstition and abuses of state power – some claimed the Illuminati were responsible for the French Revolution; [Latin plural of *illuminatus* (enlightened)]; [historical]

illuminative having the power to produce light; causing illumination; tending to illustrate; [adj.]; [synonym: *illustrative*]; "Those dreams are coherent, rational, sometimes *illuminative*."
– Annie Besant, *The Changing World*, 1909

illusory deceptive; imaginary; not real; [adj.]; [Spanish *ilusorio* illusory]; "'I despise your books ...

It is all worthless, fleeting, *illusory*, and deceptive, like a mirage.'" – Anton Chekhov, *The Bet*, 1889

illutible describing that which cannot be cleansed or erased; [very rare adj.]; [Latin *lōtus* washed]

imbastardize to bastardize; to make illegitimate; to debase; [verb]

imitatrix (pl. *imitatrices*) a female imitator; [noun]; [synonym: *imitatress*]; [Latin]

immantle to cover; to mantle; [verb]; "the forested hills, *immantled* in a soft, golden light..."

Immelmann maneuver or **roll-off-the-top** an aircraft maneuver that results in level flight at a higher altitude; [noun]; [Max *Immelmann*, German WWI flying ace]

immingle to mix; to mingle; to blend; [verb]; "*immingling* vapors"

impalpable not able to be sensed or perceived, esp. by the sense of touch; not easily understood; [adj.]; [synonym: *intangible*]; [Spanish *palpar* (to touch; to feel)]; "It was like the phantasmagoria of delirium, utterly *impalpable*, but yet intensely real." – Maria L. Ramé, *Cecil Castlemaine's Gage*, 1900

impenitent not penitent; unrepentant; not willing or able to change one's bad or sinful behavior; [adj.]; [synonym: *obdurate*]

imperatrix (pl. *imperatrices*) an empress; a female supreme ruler; [rare & archaic]; [Latin]

imperdible indestructible; [obsolete adj.]; [Spanish *perder* (to lose; to waste)]

imperial cave salamander a species of salamander living in Sardinia; [AKA *scented cave salamander*]

imperious arrogant or domineering; [adj.]; "She was quick, beautiful, *imperious,* while he was quiet, slow, and misty." – Stephen Crane, *The Angel Child*, 1899

implausibility the collective term for *gnus*, AKA *wildebeest* – an even-toed horned ungulate native to Eastern and Southern Africa

implumed without plumes or feathers; [adj.]; [synonym: *featherless*]; [Lithuanian *plùnksna* (feather, quill)]; "Prematurely forced into flight, the fledgling – so recently *implumed* – floundered at first, yet somehow remained aloft..."

improbity a lack of integrity; dishonesty; [noun]; [Italian *probo* honesty]

impuissant weak; feeble; impotent; [adj.]; [French *puissant* powerful]

in flagrante delicto in the very act of committing a crime or other misdeed; while engaged in sexual activity; [adverb]; [synonym: *red-handed*]; [Medieval Latin, literally: *while the crime is blazing*]

in silico in computer simulation; done in virtual reality; [rare]; [modeled after *in vitro* – in a test tube]; [Latin *silex* stone]; "She had only landed aircraft *in silico* – never in real life."

in statu nascendi emerging but not yet fully developed; nascent; [adj.]; [Latin, literally: *in a state of being born*]

inaniloquent given to silly or pointless speech; [adj.]; [very rare synonym: *inaniloquous*]; [Spanish *inane* pointless]; "The children seemed intelligent, yet also particularly *inaniloquent.*"

incarnadine colored a pale pinkish-red; crimson; having a red color; the color of raw flesh; blood-stained; [adj. & noun]; [archaic & literary]

indecorous rude; in bad taste; lacking propriety; not suitable for polite society; [adj.]; [antonym: *decorous*]

Indira Point a village located at the southernmost point in all of India on Great Nicobar Island; [named after *Indira* Gandhi – formerly known as Pygmalion Point]

Indo-Gangetic Plain a 172-million-acre fertile plain bounded on the north by the Himalayas and incl. parts of India, Pakistan, Nepal, most of Bangladesh, and the large cities of Delhi, Dhaka, Lahore, and Karachi

indri a type of large lemur native to Madagascar – the only known mammal other than humans that employs rhythm in their singing; [synonym: *babakoto*]

inesculent inedible; [adj.]; "We could catch one, Tom said, and eat it raw. Though rats are as they say *inesculent*. The learned word bounced hollowly." – Anthony Burgess, *A Dead Man in Deptford*, 1993

infandous extremely odious; unnatural and reviled; [obsolete adj.]; [Latin *īnfandus* unspeakable]

ing a pasture or meadow, esp. a low one near a river; [Scots, Danish, and Norwegian *eng* meadow]

ingleside beside a dwelling's fireplace; [Scotland]; "They gathered *ingleside* and burnt the last of the furniture."

ingurgitate to eat or drink greedily and/or in large quantity; to guzzle; to engorge; [verb];

[synonym: *gorge*]; [Latin *gurges* whirlpool];
"rude, *ingurgitating* dinner guests"

inimitable better than any imitation; matchless;
[adj.]; [antonym: *imitable*];
"...he had the most picturesque and *inimitable*
vocabulary of vituperation..."
– Miriam A. DeFord, *Laureate of Bohemia*, 1947

innubilous cloudless; [very rare adj.];
[synonym: *severe clear*]; [antonym: *nubilous*];
[Welsh *nudd* haze]; "sailing under *innubilous* skies"

inordinate excessive; extreme; in greater
magnitude than is reasonable or appropriate;
[adj.]; [synonyms: *overmuch* & *intemperate*];
"*inordinate* desires"

inquietude a state of being restless or nervous;
[noun]; [antonym: *quietude*]

inquisitorial pertaining to the *Inquisition*; like an
inquisition; in the manner of a rigorous and
unfriendly inquiry; [adj.]; "*inquisitorial* interviews"

insatiate incapable of being satisfied; forever
hungry; very greedy; [literary adj.]; [antonym:
satiable]; "For glory, she was *insatiate*..."

insensate not having consciousness; inanimate;
foolish; irrational; unfeeling; heartless; [adj.];
[first def. antonym: *sentient*]; [Italian *insensato*
senseless]

insouciant carefree; nonchalant; [adj.]; [French
souciant worrying]; "Handsome, *insouciant*,
always agreeable and of a curious dignity of
carriage he seemed cut out to be a King."
– Flora Annie Steel, *King-Errant*, 1912

intarsia a decorative style of Italian wood inlaying –
   sometimes contrasting with ivory or bone;
   [synonym: *marquetry*]

inter alia among other things; [adverb]; [synonym:
   et alia]; [Latin]

interfluent flowing between (or into) one another;
   [rare adj.]; *"interfluent streams"*

interfluve an area of high ground between two
   connected river valleys; [noun]; [geology]

interfulgent shining between or through; [rare adj.];
   "Is there not enchantment for the eyes of
   the metaphysician in this play of light, these
   nameless *interfulgent* colours which appear
   flimsy as the play of thought?"
   – Louis Bertrand, *Saint Augustin*, 1914

interior locution a mystical concept and type of
   private revelation wherein a person receives
   supernatural communication to the ears, the
   imagination, or directly to their cognitive faculty

interleave or **interleaf** to insert something, esp.
   blank pages, between a book's pages; to
   intersperse something, esp. at regular intervals,
   between parts of another thing; [verb]

Intermontane Islands a roughly 700-mile chain of
   island volcanoes that eventually drifted into
   North America 180 million years BCE to form part
   of British Columbia – the islands were too big to
   sink below so they melded onto the continent,
   forming the *Intermontane Belt*

iracund angry; irritable; [rare adj.]; [synonym:
   choleric]; [Italian & Spanish *ira* anger]

iridal pertaining to rainbows; [rare adj.];
   [Ancient Greek *îris* rainbow]; *"iridal colors"*

iron catastrophe a hypothesized geological event relatively early in Earth's history during which iron, nickel, and other heavy metals migrated to the Earth's core; the core then became a large spinning mass of super-heated metal that in turn created the Earth's magnetic field, protecting the atmosphere from being stripped away by solar wind and shielding life from harmful radiation

iron-hearted cruel; pitiless; rigidly unsympathetic; [adj.]; "*iron-hearted* despots"

iron star a hypothetical type of compact star that has been transmuted into iron – could occur 10^{1500} years from now

irreality unreality; [rare noun]; "That sense of *irreality* which had struck him on his first view of the island was still persisting;" – Norman Douglas, *South Wind*, 1917

isochasm a line connecting locations with the same frequency of auroras; [Ancient Greek *ísos* equal + *khásma* abyss]

isochronal or **isochronic** of equal duration; happening at regular intervals; [adj.]; [synonym: *isochronous*]; [Greek *ísos* equal]

isogloss the actual geographic boundary (or the line on a map so delineating) of a particular linguistic feature – e.g., a vowel's pronunciation; [noun]

isohel a line on a map linking locations that receive equal amounts of sunshine, measured either in total solar radiation or in daily hours; [noun]; [Ancient Greek *hélios* (sun, east, sunshine)]; "Each map shows a zone of increased sunshine between Ghana and Nigeria, destroying the regular pattern of east-west trending *isohels*

across southern Nigeria and Ivory Coast."
– Derek Hayward, *Climatology of West Africa*, 1987
ivied covered with a climbing plant, esp. ivy; [adj.];
"...he was broodingly unable to see even the most
ivied tower as anything but a pile of stones till,
inexplicably, the miracle of recovered hope and
courage transformed him."
– Sinclair Lewis, *World So Wide*, 1951

J

jacinth (JAY-sinth) a translucent, reddish variety
of the mineral zircon – used as a gemstone;
a *hyacinth* – the bulbous, flowering plant native
to South Africa & the Mediterranean; [noun];
[Middle English *jacynct* sapphire]
Jackson Pollocks testicles; [rare noun];
[Cockney rhyming slang for *bollocks*]
jardinière a planter; an ornamental container, esp.
a pot, for displaying flowers; [noun]; [French]
Jasper Seamount an underwater volcano in the
Pacific Ocean west of Baja California
jazzy in a jazzlike style; flashy; showy; jittery or
jangly; [adj.]; "Her dress was variegated, sequined,
and structurally complex – quite *jazzy*."
Jebel Musa a Moroccan mountain that, along with
the Rock of Gibraltar, flanks the entrance to the
Mediterranean Sea – together anciently known
as the *Pillars of Hercules*; [Arabic *Jabal Mūsā*
(Mount Moses)]
jejunum (pl. *jejuna*) the middle section of the small
intestine, between the *ileum* and *duodenum*;
[noun]; [Latin *iēiūnum* (fasting, hungry)]

Jenny Greenteeth a long-haired river-hag with green skin and sharp teeth – the creature pulls children and the aged into water to drown them; [English folklore]

Jesus boots sandals; [UK slang]

jobbernowl or **jabbernowl** a blockhead; [noun]; [French *jobard* (stupid, gullible)]

joie de vivre the simple joy of living; an enthusiasm for life; [noun]; [French *joy of living*]; "He was the strongest type of person – cascading tragedies seemed not to blunt his natural *joie de vivre*."

jouissance pleasure; orgasm; [very rare noun]; [French]

Jovian trojans a group of thousands of known asteroids that share Jupiter's orbit around the Sun – about one million such asteroids over 1 km in diameter are estimated to exist; [each named after a figure from the *Trojan War* in Greek myth. – the first discovered was *588 Achilles* in 1906]

jugerum or **juger** an ancient Roman unit of area equal to about ¼ hectare

jugular notch or **Plender gap** the roughly v-shaped dip between the clavicles and above the sternum

jugum penis or **pollutions ring** a male anti-masturbation device consisting of a metal ring with serrated teeth – invented in the Victorian era (1700s); [Portuguese *jugo* yoke]

julienne cut into long, thin strips (of vegetables); to cut vegetables in this way; the vegetables cut thusly; a soup with *julienned* vegetables added; [adj., verb, and noun]

jump the shark when a creative work (often a TV show or streaming series) has reached a point where its core intent has been exhausted and new ideas are discordant with the original purpose, style, or effect; [coined in 1985 based on a 1977 episode of *Happy Days* in which Fonzi jumps a shark on water skis]; "We were really loving that show, but it *jumped the shark* in the third season."

K

Kali or **Kalika** a Hindu goddess associated with time, creation, destruction, and death – she destroys evil and protects the innocent; Shiva's consort, she has blue skin, four arms, wears a necklace of severed heads, and is accompanied by serpents and a jackal; [AKA *Kali Mata* (the dark mother)]

kalokagathia a Platonic teaching promoting the harmonious combination of physical, moral, and spiritual virtues to achieve a chivalrous ideal of excellence in noble fighting, speech, and song; [Ancient Greek *kalós kaì agathós* (beautiful & good)]

Kalpavriksha a wish-fulfilling divine tree in several Indic religions; [Sanskrit *aeon tree*]

karaburan a hot and dusty named wind of Central Asia; [Turkmen *black storm*]

Karatgurk seven sisters representing the seven stars in the constellation Pleiades – the *Karatgurk* alone possessed the secret of fire and each carried a live coal; [Australian Aboriginal myth.]

Karelian Bear Dog a Finnish breed named for its ability to hunt Eurasian brown bears, but also used to hunt lynx, moose, and wolves – viewed by many Finns as a national treasure;

[*Karelia*, a northern European region that includes parts of Russia & Finland]

karuṇā universal, loving compassion; a significant spiritual concept in several Indic religions; [Sanskrit *karuṇā* (compassion, spiritual longing)]

katzbalger a short, stout sword sometimes used by archers when forced to fight too close for bows; the signature blade of the *Lansquenets* – Germanic mercenaries of the Renaissance era; [perhaps from German *Katze* (cat) + *balgen* (brawling) to suggest cat-like intense fighting in close quarters]

keratogenesis the formation of *keratin* – the protein that makes up hair and nails; [noun]; [adj. *keratogenic*]; [Greek *kéras* horn]

Kickapoo an Algonquian-speaking Native American tribe originating in an area south of the Great Lakes; [Kickapoo possibly means *wanderer*]

Kidlington a large village in Oxfordshire, England

kismet or **kismat** fate; destiny, esp. if unavoidable; [synonym: *fortune*]; [Arabic *qisma* (dividing, destiny)]; "But at this point fickle *Kismet*, who for a day had played with him bitterly and sardonically, decided to reward him in full for the amusement he had afforded her." – F. Scott Fitzgerald, *The Camel's Back*, 1920

knell to toll; to ring slowly, as for a funeral; [verb]; [Old English *cnyllan* (to strike, to knock)]

knight-errant or **knight-erratic** (pl. *knights-erratic*) a knight, esp. as dipicted in medieval romances, gallivanting about the country in search of adventure and a chance to prove his chivalry; a person with an adventurous spirit who is also highly idealistic; "... the strangest notion that ever madman in this world hit upon... for the service of his country... he should make a *knight-errant* of himself, roaming the world... on horseback in quest of adventures... righting every kind of wrong, and exposing himself to peril and danger" – John Ormsby, *Don Quixote* (translated from Cervantes), 1885

knight of the plume a writer; [rare noun]; [synonym: *litterateur*]

Koch snowflake one of the earliest discovered *fractal curves*; [20th c. Swedish mathematician Helge von *Koch*]

kompromat information suitable for blackmail, esp. in a Russian context; evidence that someone doesn't want to come to light; [Russian *kompromát* (short for *compromising material*) – KGB slang from the time of Stalin]

Kraken galaxy a hypothetical galaxy theorized to have collided with our galaxy (*the Milky Way*) eleven billion years ago

Kreutz sungrazers sun-grazing comets with orbits very closely approaching the sun at *perihelion*; [German astronomer Heinrich *Kreutz*]

Kubrickian relating to, or made in the manner of, Stanley Kubrick, 20th c. American film director noted for his technical perfectionism and atmospheric visual styles; [rare adj.]

Kuiper belt a circumstellar, donut-shaped disk in the outer Solar System composed of frozen matter and rock & metal asteroids – similar to the asteroid belt, but much larger; consists of over 100,000 objects beyond the orbit of Neptune,

many over 100km in diameter, incl. the dwarf
planet Pluto; [Dutch astronomer Gerard *Kuiper*]

kumari kandam a lost continent in the Indian
Ocean – supposedly home to an ancient Tamil
civilization; [Tamil *kumari* maiden + *kandam*
continent]

Kungurian age an age within the *Permian* geologic
period about 283-273 million years BCE; [named
after the Russian city of *Kungur*]

kurgan esp. in Siberia and Central Asia, a type of
prehistoric *tumulus* (a burial mound covering a
grave) – often contains a single body, weapons,
and horses; [Ukrainian *kurhan* (fortress, high
grave)]

kyphorrhinos describing a nose that is humped or
has a bump; [very rare adj.]; [Ancient Greek
kúphos (humpback, bent)]

L

labial scales the scales around the mouth of any
species of scaled reptile, esp. snakes – the two
types of such scales are *supralabials* and
sublabials; [Spanish *labio* lip]

labyrinthine like a labyrinth; very *tortuous* – windy
and maze-like; [synonyms: *labyrinthic*, *labyrinthial*,
labyrinthian]; [Russian *labirínt* labyrinth];
"The whimsically travelled hedge-paths and
greenways *labyrinthine* – from pond to pasturage,
from stream-bridge to wood..."

lacrimae rerum the inherent tragedy or sadness of
human existence; [Latin, literally: *tears of things*];
[Italian *lacrima* tear];

"There are *lacrimae rerum* and mortal things touch the mind." – Virgil, *Aeneid*, circa 25 BCE

lacrimal lake a pool of tears in the lower eye upstream of the tear drainage system – usually holds 7-10 microliters (cubic milliliters) of tears

lactiferous able to secrete milk or a milk-like substance; [adj.]; [Spanish *lactado* breastfed]

Lacus Oblivionis a small *lunar mare* (a dark, basaltic plain) on the Moon; [Latin *Lake of Forgetfulness*]

lakehead the area of a lake that is farthest from its outlet; [rare noun]

La-La Land nickname for *Los Angeles*, California and *British Columbia*, Canada; [humorous slang]

lachrymose sad; sorrowful; relating to tears; pertaining to the act of weeping; [adj.]; [synonym: *lacrimal*]; [antonym: *unlachrymose*]; [Old Latin *dacrima* tear]

lactogenesis the secretion of milk by the mammary glands of a female mammal, including humans; [rare noun]

lady garden a woman's pubic area; [UK slang]

Lakshadweep an Indian archipelago of 36 islands in the Arabian Sea; [synonym: *Laccadive Islands*]; [Sanskrit *lakṣadvīpa* (hundred thousand islands)]

lalochezia the use of vulgar language to ease stress; [rare noun]; [German *lallen* (to babble)]; [Ancient Greek *khézō* (to defecate)]

lamentation the collective term for swans; "The drifting *lamentation* of swans, pure and white..."

lamster a fugitive from the law on the run; [rare noun]; [slang]; [English *lam* (to flee)]

landreeve an assistant to the steward of a large estate: "At nearly midnight the *landreeve* remembered he'd not locked the farthest gate..."

landscape zodiac a supposed map of the stars formed by landscape features, both built and natural – an alleged example *Temple of the Stars* in Somerset, England, has been scientifically debunked

lapidate to throw stones or other dangerous objects at a person in punishment; to verbally insult someone, esp. with dramatic brutality; [verb]; [synonym: *to stone*]

lapis lazuli a deep-blue metamorphic rock prized for its intense color; of a deep, bright blue color; [noun & adj.]; [Medieval Latin *lapis* (stone) + *lazulī* (azure, sky)]; "I cannot convey to you the sheer and surreal scale of everything: the towering ship, the ropes, the ties, the anchor, the pier, the vast *lapis lazuli* dome of the sky." – David Foster Wallace, *A Supposedly Fun Thing I'll Never Do Again*, 1997

lapsus calami a mistake in writing, esp. when hand-written; [synonym: *lapsus plumae*]; [Italian *calamo* quill]; [Latin, literally: *slip of the pen*]

Laputan fanciful; absurd; describing an obviously impractical idea proposed in philosophy or science; [adj.]; [from *Laputa* – a flying island in Jonathan Swift's *Gulliver's Travels*, 1726]

lardaceous resembling lard or pig-fat; having excess fat; [adj.]; [Old French *lard* bacon]; "The tunnel walls were warm and soft, and coated with a claggy substance, thick and *lardaceous*."

larvated masked or wearing something mask-like; containing larvae; [adj.]; [Latin *lārva* (ghost, demon, mask)]

lassitude lethargy; fatigue; listlessness; [noun]; [synonym: *languor*]; [Italian & Portuguese *lasso* (weak, very tired)]; "The heat increased his *lassitude* and led to long, languid days lying in late and rising only to loll about in lengthening shadow."

lasslorn or **lass-lorn** forsaken by one's lass or mistress; [archaic adj.]; [Middle English *lorn* lost]; "Bless'd hope, when Tempe takes her last long flight, And leaves her *lass-lorn* lover to complain, Like Luna mantling o'er the brow of night, Thy glowing wing dispels the gloom of pain."
– George Horton, *To Miss Tempe*, 1845

latibulum (pl. *latibula*) a hidden lair or place to hide; a burrow; [rare noun]; [Latin *lateō* (to hide)]; "To your *latibulum* go and hide; Hide for decades, if you dare – I await you next century in the open air."

lattermath (pl. *lattermaths*) the second mowing; figuratively, the later consequences or developments; [noun]; [synonym: *aftermath*]

lazuline of a pale blue color; [rare adj.]; [Latin *lazulum* (heaven, sky)]; "beneath *lazuline* skies"

leaflitter or **leaf litter** fallen dead plant material piled on the ground, esp. leaves, twigs, and bark; "Imagine: flowing rivers and warm, halcyon summers. Did the leaves of this tree flutter in a wind that blew off a temperate sea? Did birds forage in its boughs by day; did marsupials

snuffle in its *leaf litter* by night?"
– David Campbell, *The Crystal Desert...*, 2002

legislatrix (pl. *legislatrices*) a female legislator; [archaic & rare]; [synonym: *legislatress*]; [Latin]; "Three newly-elected *legislatrices* walk into a bar..."

lemon drop mangosteen or **monkey fruit** a tasty tropical fruit, the tree of which is native to Central America; [noun]

lenticular cloud or **lenticularis** a stationary cloud that forms in the *troposphere*, usually in parallel alignment with the wind direction – often shaped like a lens or a flying saucer; [Latin *lenticula* lentil]

Levant, the the Eastern Mediterranean area, usually referring to Syria, Cyprus, Israel, Jordan, Lebanon, Palestine, and part of Turkey; but also sometimes incl. all or parts of Greece, Iraq, Libya, Turkey, and Egypt; [adj. *Levantine*]; [Italian *levante* rising]; "*Levantine* cuisine"

Levanter, the a Mediterranean wind that blows west through the Strait of Gibraltar

Levantine Sea, the the eastern part of the Mediterranean Sea; the sea east of the Libyan Sea

lexiphanic writing or speaking in a way that is intended to impress others; bombastic; [adj.]; [synonym: *magniloquent*]; [from *Lexiphanes,* a character created by 2nd c. Syrian satirist *Lucian of Samosata*]; "*lexiphanic* lectures"

librocubicularist a person that enjoys reading in bed; [rare]; [Latin *cubiculum* (small bedroom)]

Library of Pergamum a library founded in the 3rd c. BCE in what is now western Turkey – holding 200,000 volumes, the library was in fierce competition with the *Great Library of Alexandria,*

which was founded about a century earlier;
[historical]

Liburnia in historical geography, a coastal region
home to the ancient *Liburni* tribe – the region is
now part of Croatia

liegeless not having a lord or master; [adj.];
[archaic & poetic]

lightfast resistant to fading; [rare adj.];
[synonyms: *colorfast* & *sunfast*]

light-mantled albatross a species of albatross
native to the Southern Ocean

Lima syndrome a hostage situation in which
abductors begin to feel sympathy with their
hostages; [rare noun]; [antonym: *Stockholm
Syndrome*]; [hundreds were taken hostage at a
1996 Japanese embassy party in *Lima*, Peru]

liminal of or relating to an entrance; relating to the
start of a process; [adj.]; [2nd def. synonyms:
inceptive & *inchoative*]

limitrophe bordering; a border area; [adj. & noun];
[rare]; [Italian *limitrofa* bordering]

limpid clear and bright; transparent; easy to
understand; [adj.]; "The *limpid* and spiritless
vacuity of this intellectual jellyfish is in ludicrous
contrast with the rude but robust mental activities
that he came to quicken and inspire."
– Ambrose Bierce, 1882 (describing Oscar Wilde)

lines of Blaschko, the stripes present on all humans
and many other animals – usually only visible
under ultraviolet light; [Alfred *Blaschko*, 20th c.
German doctor]

lingula a tongue-shaped fleshy or bony structure;
[noun]; [adj. *lingular*]; [Latin *small tongue*];

"... a poisonous alien creature bristling with diverse *lingular* appendages."

lisztomania historically, the intense fan frenzy for the music of Hungarian composer Franz Liszt; [rare noun]; [coined by German poet Heinrich Heine as *Lisztomanie* in 1844]

liturgy a written or predetermined set of rituals to be performed, esp. during a Christian religious service; [adj. *liturgic*]; [Ancient Greek *lāós* (people assembled)]

locus (pl. *loci*) a specific place or location, esp. if the center of activity; [Italian *luogo* location]; "The kitchen so often plays the *locus*, the most crowded center, of American house parties."

locus amoenus (pl. *loci amoeni*) an idealized place of safety and ease with grass, trees, and some type of water body; a classic literary setting that is often a mysterious, feminine place away from rigid societal norms such as the Shakespearean "green world" of *A Midsummer Night's Dream*; [rare noun]; [Latin *pleasant place*]

logomachy a battle of words; an intense, but verbal-only, conflict; [noun]; [synonym: *war of words*]; "Their *logomachy* was far more stimulating to his intellect than the reserved and quiet dogmatism of Mr. Morse." – Jack London, *Martin Eden*, 1909

London Beer Flood an 1814 flood of about ¼ million gallons of beer released when a large wooden vat of fermenting porter burst – eight people in a neighboring slum were killed; [historical]

looky-loo a too-interested bystander; a gawker; a nosy person; "The loud argument spilled into the street, and soon the inevitable, always unwelcome *looky-loos* appeared..."

loose unit a person that is *off the rails* or out of control and unpredictable; a person whose actions are very stupid, damaging, or disrespectful, esp. if obviously and brazenly so; [rare noun]; [Australian slang]

Lost Gardens of Heligan gardens in Cornwall, England created in the mid-18th c. – neglected during WWI and restored in the 1990s

Lost Generation, **the** the generation that was in early adulthood during WWI, many of which were at least perceived as being directionless and disoriented during the early postwar period; a group of American expat writers residing in Paris during the 1920s; [proper noun]; [coined by 20th c. American writer Gertrude Stein]; "You are all a *lost generation*." – Hemingway's epigraph to *The Sun Also Rises*, 1926

lotusland a place that induces contentment by seeming to be idyllic; a soft and easy place populated by pleasure-seekers; [noun]; [from the legendary island of the lotus-eaters in Homer's *Odyssey*]; [Latin *lōtum* (washed, elegant)]

Loveridge's sunbird a species of Tanzanian bird that favors a tropical moist montane forest habitat; [Arthur *Loveridge*, 20th c. British biologist]

lucent shining; luminous; spreading light; [adj.]; [Latin *lūx* light]; "...his *lucent* goodness, which provoked answering devotion even from the depraved, made him the only leader (and a benediction) for forlorn hopes." – T. E. Lawrence (of Arabia), *Seven Pillars of Wisdom*, 1926

lucre money or riches, esp. if ill-gotten or having a corrupting effect; [noun]; [Latin *lucrum* profit]; "...only fair that you should pocket the *lucre*. I've had my share already." – Robert Louis Stevenson, *The Body Snatcher*, 1884

ludography a list of select games; a video game (or boardgame) designer's body of work; [rare noun]; "The immersive artist's *ludography* included no other work so boldly creative, so Promethean..."

ludomania a severe addiction to gambling; [very rare noun]; [Latin *lūdō* (I play)]

ludophilia the love of play; [very rare noun]; [French *ludique* playful]; "The Zeitgeist was one of insouciant *ludophilia*..."

lumiere green sky green; [rare noun]; [French *lumière* light]

luminary one who has achieved success, esp. in an artistic or scientific field; [noun]

lumpenintelligentsia the lowest echelon of the *intelligentsia* (society's intellectual elite); [very rare noun]; [German *lumpen* rag]; [according to 19th c. German political philosopher Karl Marx]

lunar mare (pl. *lunar maria*); one of 22 large, dark basaltic plains on the Moon; [Latin *maria* seas]

lushington a drunkard of the first order; a lush; [rare]; "Small blood vessels ruptured in the cheeks of *lushingtons*, pressed on the chilly pillow of a curb." – Alan Moore, English comic book writer

Lusosphere or **Lusofonia** the 300 million people that speak Portuguese; the countries or provinces in which most of these people reside, including Portugal, Brazil, Uruguay, Goa, Angola,

Mozambique, *et alia*; [Latin *Lusitania* (an ancient Iberian province)]

Lyman-alpha blobs concentrations of gas that can reach over 400,000 light years across – some of the universe's largest known individual objects; [astronomy]

lyre-tailed honeyguide a species of bird endemic to the African tropical rainforest

lysergic hallucinatory; psychedelic; [rare adj.]; "*lysergic* films"

M

MacGyver to fix or create something using unconventional means or materials, esp. doing so with ingenious improvisation; [rare verb]; [adj. *MacGyverian*]; [synonym: *jury-rig*]; [American TV series *MacGyver*]; "Her *MacGyverian* desert repair of the Landcruiser may have literally saved their lives."

macrosomatous having a very large physical body; [very rare adj.]; [Ancient Greek *sôma* body]

Mad Gasser, **the** the moniker of a person purported to be guilty of over 20 gas attacks over two weeks in 1944 in Mattoon, Illinois; victims reported strange smells and various unpleasant symptoms – causal theories include industrial pollution, mass hysteria, or even a real *mad gasser*; [historical]

mad honey honey produced from certain pollens and nectars (including those of some species of *Rhododendron*) that has hallucinogenic effects when consumed by humans but is also mildly to severely toxic – such honey is deliberately

produced in Nepal and the Black Sea region
of Turkey

Mad River Glen a ski area in Vermont, America

madchester a genre of alternative rock (and
its attendant cultural scene) developed in
Manchester, UK in the late 1980s – influenced
by indie, psychedelic, and dance music and incl.
bands like *Happy Mondays* and *The Stone Roses*;
[*mad + Manchester*]

madder crimson a vivid red color; [rare noun]

madding raging; furious; affected with madness;
[archaic adj.]; "...arms on armour clashing bray'd
Horrible discord, and the *madding* wheels
Of brazen chariots raged;"
– Milton, *Paradise Lost*, 1667

madescent becoming damp or moist; slightly damp;
[rare adj.]; [Latin *madeō* (I am moist, I am drunk)];
"As she tasted the wine, her *madescent* skin
seemed to gleam in the warm evening sun."

Madrean sky islands 27 relatively small enclaves
of the greater *Madrean pine-oak woodlands*
biogeographic region – the *sky islands* are
located in mountain ranges in Arizona, New
Mexico, and Texas

madrigal a short poem that is easily set
to music and often pastoral in nature;
[noun]; [adjectives: *madrigalian & madrigalic*]

maelid a nymph associated with apple trees; [rare
noun]; [Greek myth.]; [Italian *meli* (apple trees)]

maelstrom the collective term for a group of
salamanders

magma (pl. *magmata*) the molten material under
the Earth's crust from which lava flows; any soft,

heavy, dough-like mass; the residuum left after juicing fruits; [noun]; [adj. *magmatic*]

magnetogravitic in physics, of or relating to the hypothetical combined effects of magnetism and gravity; [rare adj.]; [synonym: *gravitomagnetic*]

maleficium (pl. *maleficia*) an act of magic intended to cause harm to persons or property; [noun]; [archaic & very rare]; [Latin]; [Italian *malefico* evil]; "In the 14th century *maleficium* was one of the charges made against the Knights Templar by the Kingdom of France – many were subsequently burned at the stake."

malloseismic an area likely to undergo several or more large earthquakes per century; of or relating to such an area; [noun & adj.]; [very rare]

mammiferous mammalian; having *mammae* or breasts; [adj.]; [synonym: *mammillate*]

mammoth steppe or **steppe-tundra** during the Last Glacial Maximum this was Earth's most extensive biome, stretching west to east from the Iberian Peninsula, across Asia, through Beringia (Alaska) and Canada; a cold, expansive, mostly flat grassland home to these species, *inter alia*: herbivores: reindeer, saiga antelope, yak, steppe bison, woolly rhinoceros, and woolly mammoth; carnivores: bears, cave lions, scimitar cats, wolverines, and wolves

mamzer or **mamser** a child born outside marriage; a detestable person; [noun]; [Yiddish *momzer*; literally: a bastard]

mandakranta a type of poetical meter in classic Sanskrit poetry; first employed by Kalidasa,

as in his famous poem *The Cloud-Messenger*;
[noun]; [Sanskrit *slow-stepping*]

manky disgustingly dirty; [adj.]; [synonym: *grufted*]

manqueller executioner; murderer; manslayer;
a killer of men; [obsolete noun]

manumit to release from slavery; to liberate from
personal bondage or servitude; to free; [verb];
[noun: *manumission*]; [synonym: *liberate*]

Map of Africa, **The** the Africa-shaped, seaward
entrance to the *Caves of Hercules* in Morocco –
likely created by the Phoenicians

map lichen a type of lichen that grows on rocks in
mountainous regions and often resembles a map

marcel a distinct, wavy hairstyle created using a
curling iron; styling hair in such a manner; [noun
& verb]; [synonym: *marcel wave*]; [from the given
French name *Marcel*]; "Her hair was auburn, with
a prominent *marcel wave*."

Mare Nubium a *lunar mare* (a dark, basaltic
plain) on the Moon's near side; [Latin *sea of
clouds*]

Mare Spumans a dark, basaltic plain on the Moon's
near side; [Latin *foaming sea*]

Mare Tenebrosum a name for the Atlantic Ocean
in the Middle Ages; [Latin *dark sea*]

marginalia notes in the margins of a document,
draft, or book; [noun]; [synonym: *apostils*];
[Latin *margō* (border, edge)]

Marian apparition a supposed supernatural
appearance of *Mary* – the mother of Jesus

Marlenesque characteristic of Marlene Dietrich,
20th c. German-American actress and singer;
highly successful, she was known for

androgynous film roles; [very rare adj.];
"Her voice was deep and resonant – in a word:
Marlenesque."

Mashriq, **the** or **the Mashrek** Arabic term for the
eastern Arab world: Bahrain, Jordan, Iraq, Iran,
Kuwait, Egypt, Oman, Yemen, Lebanon, Palestine,
Qatar, Saudi Arabia, Sudan, Syria, and UAE;
[antonym: *Maghreb* – the western part of North
Africa]; [Arabic *sharaqa* (to shine, to rise)]

masked water tyrant a species of South American
bird in the family Tyrinnidae

mathematical beauty the experience of aesthetic
pleasure that leads some to describe mathematics
as beautiful or as a creative activity with similar
aspects to music & poetry; [noun]

Maunder Minimum a period from 1645 to 1715 CE
(during the Little Ice Age) when less than 50
sunspots were observed – about 45,000 sunspots
are typically observed during modern times over
a similar timeframe; [20th c. English solar
astronomers Edward & Annie *Maunder*]

Max Headroom Incident in 1987 the TV signals
of two Chicago stations were hijacked to air
a recording of someone dressed like *Max
Headroom*, a fictional TV character – the culprits
remain unknown; [historical]

Mead of Poetry or **Poetic Mead** a beverage that
endows a type of omniscience upon any who
drink of it – a metaphor for poetic inspiration;
[Norse myth.]

meadowed having meadows; [adj.];
"The *meadowed* memories of her sunlit youth..."

Megatherium an extinct genus of South American ground sloth – one species was elephant-sized; [Greek *thirío* beast]

melancholic filled with deep sadness or depression, esp. of an introspective nature; a person who is often melancholy or has a sad and subdued nature; [adj. & noun]; "Pantagruel seemed metagrabolized, dozing, out of sorts, and as *melancholic* as a cat." – François Rabelais, *Gargantua and Pantagruel*, 1552

Melanesia a subregion of Oceania NE of Australia that extends from New Guinea to Fiji; [adj. *Melanesian*]; [Ancient Greek *mélas* dark + *nêsos* islands]

melanocomous having dark or black hair; [rare adj.]; [Greek *melanós* (dark, black)]

mellific producing honey; [adj.]; [Latin *mellis* honey]

melodic death metal or **melodeath** a subgenre of *death metal* that includes melodic or harmonized guitar riffs and often high-pitched shrieking vocals as well as the low-pitched growls common in traditional *death metal*

melton a thick, tough, and smooth fabric often traditionally used for overcoats; [*Melton Mowbray* – an English town]

memelord a person who often creates and spreads *memes* – usually humorous, Internet-distributed material; [rare noun]; [Internet slang]

meme pool all the *memes* (transmittable units of cultural ideas) present in a given human population; "Just as genes propagate themselves in the gene pool by leaping from body to body via sperms or eggs, so memes propagate

themselves in the *meme pool* by leaping from brain to brain via a process which, in the broad sense, can be called imitation."
– Richard Dawkins, *The Selfish Gene*, 1976

memoried full of memories; having a memory; [rare adj.]; [poetic & literary]; "the *memoried* ruins of her life upon the island, long ago ..."

memory palace or **method of loci** a strategy for memory enhancement wherein one visualizes a familiar spatial environment in order to aid information recall; [noun]

memosphere the sphere of human communication (esp. social media) wherein *memes* (transmitted ideas, often humorous) are distributed; [very rare noun]

meracious pure; without adulteration; unmixed; strong; [very rare adj.]; [Latin *merus* pure]

meridional southern; in the south; like southern people, esp. those in southern Europe; [adj.]; [Spanish *meridiem* (midday, noon)]

mesmeric relating to *mesmerism*, or its methods of hypnosis; enthralling; transfixing; [adj.]; [noun: *mesmerist*]; [19th c. German physician Franz Anton *Mesmer* developed the animal magnetism theory]; "One cast of those deep, green *mesmeric* eyes overpowered any chance of refusal."

mesopelagic the pelagic zone about 200-1000 meters below the ocean's surface; the zone begins where only 1% of the sun's light penetrates the depths, and ends where there is no light; [Ancient Greek *pélagos* (open sea)]

meta self-referential, esp. in a clever, ironic, or humorous way; comparative by analogy, but at a higher level; [adj.]; [back-formed from *metaphysics*]

metacognition an awareness of one's own thought processes and of the patterns that shape them; sentience; [rare noun]; [adj. *metacognitive*]

metagrobolism concealment; mystification; obfuscation; [noun]; [humorous & rare]; [verb: *metagrobolize*];

"...the automatic *metagrobolism* of the Romish Church, when tottering and emblustricated with the gibble-gabble gibberish of this odious error and heresy, is homocentrically poised."
– François Rabelais, *Gargantua & Pantagruel*, 1552

metier or **métier** an activity pursued as a profession; a vocation; an activity that is particularly well-suited or appropriate for someone; [synonym: *forte*]; [French]

mewl to whimper or whine; to cry softly with a high-pitch; [verb]; "At first the infant,
Mewling and puking in the nurse's arms;
Then the whining school-boy,..."
– William Shakespeare, *As You Like It*, 1623

miasma a cloud of noxious gas or smoke; an unpleasant emanation; figuratively, a noxious and harmful atmosphere or influence; [noun]; [adj. *miasmic & miasmatic*]; [Ancient Greek *míasma* pollution]

milieu (pl. *milieux*) an environment or setting; a medium; a social setting; a social class or group, esp. one with members that hold a similar point of view; [French]

mingent discharging urine; [very rare adj.]; [Latin *mingō* (I urinate)]

mirrorshades mirrored sunglasses; [rare noun]

mirabile visu wonderful or amazing to see; [rare]; [interjection]; [Latin, literally: *strange to see*]

miserabilist a very unhappy person, esp. if also a believer in the virtue of being miserable; [rare noun]; [synonym: *killjoy*]

mishmosh or **mishmash** a collection of a variety of miscellaneous items; to mix together, esp. in a random, confusing, or particularly disorganized way; [noun & verb]; [synonyms: *melange* & *mingle-mangle*]

misocapnist a person that hates tobacco smoke; [rare noun]; [adj. *misocapnic*]; [Greek *kapnós* (smoke, tobacco)]

Mist one of the valkyries – attendants of Odin that guide honorably fallen warriors to *Valhalla*; [Norse myth.]; [Old Norse *mistr* (cloud, mist)]

mithril a fictional metal appearing similar to silver, but incredibly strong and very valuable; [fantasy]; [Sindarin (Tolkien-constructed language) *mith* (grey) + *ril* (glitter)]; "*Mithril*! All folk desired it. It could be beaten like copper, and polished like glass; and the Dwarves could make of it a metal, light and yet harder than tempered steel... the beauty of *mithril* did not tarnish or grow dim." – J.R.R. Tolkien, *The Fellowship of the Ring*, 1954

mizzen skysail the top sail on the aftmost mast of a three-masted, full-rigged sailing ship; [noun]; [sometimes a *moonsail* is rigged above a *skysail*]

moanworthy worthy of sorrowful moaning; worthy of lament; [very rare]; "*moanworthy* adversities"

Möbius strip in mathematics, a surface formed by giving a narrow strip a half-twist and attaching its ends; [19th c. German mathematician August Ferdinand *Möbius*]

mollitude softness; weakness; luxuriousness; [rare noun]; [Latin *mollis* soft]

molly wop to physically beat someone, esp. severely; to soundly beat someone in a game or some other contest without physical violence; [rare verb]; [Californian slang]

money-ridden dominated or very motivated by money; [rare adj.]; "a *money-ridden* culture"

monkey puzzle tree or **monkey tail tree** an evergreen pine – the national tree of Chile; [in 1850 a noted English barrister commented: "It would *puzzle* a *monkey* to climb that"]

monological pertaining to or akin to a monologue; [adj.]; "The *monological* rantings of a madman."

monstricide the killing of a monster; [rare noun]

mons veneris a rounded mass of fatty tissue over the pubic bones on a human female; [synonym: *mons pubis*]; [Latin, literally: *mount of Venus*]

montage a composite artwork created by assembling pieces of music, pictures, video, texts, etc.; [noun]; [French *montage* assembly]

moon logic logic that is very hard to understand; obtuse or quasi-logical thinking; [rare noun]; [Internet slang]

moonblood menstrual blood; [rare noun]

moonbroch or **moon-broch** a bright ring of thin cloud around the moon thought by some to herald foul weather; [obsolete noun]; [Scots]

moondust the layer of dust and sand on the Moon's surface; [noun]

moonsail a small, light sail high on the mast (above the *skysail*) employed for speed; [noun]; [synonym: *moonraker*]

moonsickle or **sickle moon** a crescent moon, esp. when thin; "*Sickle moon* just hiding in a red cloud, and the morning stars just vanished in light." – John Ruskin, *Hortus Inclusus*, 1876

moonstricken or **moonstruck** behaving irrationally, esp. in a romantic context; [adj.]

moonwashed lit by moonlight; [adj.]; [poetic & rare]; "the high, *moonwashed* rocks"

mooseyard a relatively concentrated area where moose feed in winter and snow becomes packed down; [rare noun]

moribund dying; nearing death; expiring; [adj.]; [Latin *moribunda* dying]; "Of a *moribund* star, which never more shall shine!" – Stéphane Mallarmé, 19th c. French symbolist poet

morphic resonance the theory (generally not supported by modern science) that natural systems inherit a shared memory from all previous generations and that an original idea conceived by one mind may arise in another through a mechanism similar to telepathy; [proposed by 20th c. English parapsychology researcher Alfred Rupert Sheldrake]; "The Swede's journals and research were quite closely guarded. That such strikingly Promethean theories could possibly be contemporaneously conceived by a Kiwi, half a world away, is either a wildly unlikely coincidence or evidence of *morphic resonance*."

mosaicked composed of a *mosaic* – artwork with patterned tiles that create a picture; [adj.]

mossy maze polypore a widely-distributed, inedible fungus that causes rot and decay in paper birch

mothercraft the collective skills employed during motherhood; [noun]

Mountweazel a fake entry purposely inserted into a reference work usually as a way to prove copyright infringement; [synonym: *nihilartikel*]; [from a fake entry for Lillian Virginia *Mountweazel* in the New Columbia Encyclopedia, 1975]

Mousterian Pluvial a rainy period in North Africa from about 50,000 to 30,000 BCE; [archaic]; [*Le Moustier* (French archeological site) + English *pluvial* (a rainy period)]

Moving Sands or **Flowing Sands** a supposed geographical feature included in many works over two millennia in Chinese literature – usually described as a barrier of drifting dunes or a river of sand

Mozart effect the dubious theory that listening to Mozart makes you smarter or can benefit a child's mental development

muci plural of *mucus*; [noun]

mucilaginous like mucus; slimy; [adj.]; "The cavern was smooth-floored, and randomly dotted with *mucilaginous* deposits, varying in size, shape, color, and odor."

mucoaqueous composed of both mucus and water, such as the tear film on human eyes; [rare adj.]

mucocutaneous boundary a biological region where mucus membrane transitions to skin, such as at the nostrils and lips in humans; [noun]

mucus trooper someone who comes to work even when sick; [rare noun]; [American slang]

multeity multiplicity; [rare noun]; [synonym: *manyhood*]; [Latin *multa* (much, many)]; "When the whole and the parts are seen at once, as mutually producing and explaining each other, as unity in *multeity*, there results shapeliness – *forma formosa*." – Samuel Taylor Coleridge, 1821

multisonous having many sounds, or sounding much; [adj.]; "a typically loud and *multisonous* collegiate environment"

multivagant or **multivagous** wandering often and much; [very rare adj.]; [Italian *vago* (wandering, moving)]; "Dreamers and poets are often *multivagant* by nature."

multiversant assuming many forms; [adj.]; [archaic & rare]; [synonyms: *protean* & *polymorphic*]; "The *multiversant* alien easily mimicked the Ambassador's appearance, but could not replicate her voice."

mundify to cleanse something; to purge; to purify; [very rare verb]; [Latin *munda* (clean, pure)]

munificent very generous or giving; [adj.]; [noun: *munificence*]; "So rare – a *munificent* youth!"

muriphobic afraid of rodentry, esp. mice & rats; [very rare adj.]; [Latin *mūs* (mouse, rat)]; "Although not particularly *muriphobic*, he didn't love seeing several rats while he was trying to sleep on the room's dusty floor."

murksome or **mirksome** suggestive of darkness; dark; very murky; very poorly lit; [adj.]; [synonym: *darksome*]; "...descending into *murksome* depths."

Muromian an extinct, unattested, likely Uralic language – spoken by people living in the Oka River basin in what is now western Russia; [noun]

murthering murdering; [obsolete verb]; [adj. *murtherous*]; "Those *murthering* bastards!"

mutationist an adherent of *mutationism*, a theory of biologic evolution in which mutation drives evolutionary changes rather than Darwinist natural selection; [rare noun]; [adj. *mutationistic*]

myropolist a seller of perfume; [noun]; [dated & rare]; [Greek *mýron* (sweet oil, perfume)]

mysterial enigmatic; mysterious; relating to mysteries; [adj.]; [dated & rare]

mythos (pl. *mythoi* or *mythoses*) a group of stories that have a significant meaning for a particular culture, religion, or society; a mythology; in literature, a recurring theme; [noun]

N

nacreous polar stratospheric cloud an iridescent cloud in the polar stratosphere at altitudes of 15,000 to 25,000 meters – composed of ice crystals and best observed in winter during *civil twilight*; [Middle French *nacre* (mother-of-pearl)]

Namlos a town in Austria; [German, literally: *nameless*]

Narasimha the fourth avatar of the Hindu god Vishnu – incarnated in the form of a man-lion; [Sanskrit *nara* man + *simha* lion]

nare or **naris** (pl. *nares*) a nostril; [adj. *narial*]; "There is a Machiavelian plot, Tho' ev'ry *nare* olfact it not;" – Samuel Butler, *Hudibras*, 1663

naricorn or **rhinotheca** the horn-like casing on the top of a bird's beak; [noun]

nascent emerging; just being born or entering into existence; [adj.]; [synonyms: *emergent, incipient & inchoate*]; [Old French *naistre* (to be born)]

naufrage a shipwreck, esp. when the ship is totally destroyed; [noun]; [archaic & rare]; [rare adj. *naufragous*]; [Latin *nāvis* (ship) + *frangō* (to break)]

Naughty Nineties term for the 1890s decade in the UK – marked by the plays and trial of Oscar Wilde, the supposedly decadent art of Aubrey Beardsley, various scandals, and the start of the women's voting movement; [the 1890s were known in America as the *Gay Nineties*]; [historical]

nauseant something that causes nausea, esp. certain medicines; [noun]; [synonym: *emetic*]

Nautilus a genus of nine species of mollusk with chambered shells and tentacle-like appendages known as *cirri*; [Ancient Greek *nautílos* sailor]

neathmost lowest; [rare adj.]; [synonym: *undermost*]; [UK]

Nebra sky disc a 1700 BCE bronze disc depicting the Sun, Moon, and several stars incl. the Pleiades – the disc may have been instrumental in both astronomical and religious purposes; [found buried near *Nebra,* Germany]

necrology a list of people, things, or organizations that passed on or ceased to exist over a particular period of time; an obituary or notice of a person's death; [noun]; [Ancient Greek *nekrós* dead]

Necronomicon a fictional textbook of arcane knowledge that could drive a person mad; [synonym: *Kitab al-Azif*]; [coined by H.P. Lovecraft and mentioned in several of his stories and those of other writers]

necropolis or **nekropolis** (pl. *necropoles* or *necropoli*)
a cemetary, esp. a large one in or near a city;
an ancient site used for human burials;
[adj. *necropolitan* & *necropolitic*]; "The large,
treed churchyard has a vague and unsettling
necropolitan aspect, although no graves were
reportedly present."

necropurulent necrotic and purulent – of or similar
to dead tissue issuing pus; [very rare adj.];
[Portuguese *purulenta* disgusting]

nectareal, **nectarous**, or **nectareous**
pertaining to or like nectar; sweet; [adj.];
"In the silent bliss of that purpureal twitterlight,
we sip vital elixir and taste fruits *nectareal*."

negawatt a unit of energy saved, rather than energy
expended; [rare noun]; [*negative* + *watt*]

nemeton (pl. *nemeta*) a sacred space in the ancient
Celtic religion – related placenames occur from
western Europe to central Turkey; [*Nemetona* –
a Celtic guardian goddess of open-air places of
worship]

nemorivagant wandering through a forest or a
wooded area; [very rare adj.]; [Latin *nemorivagus*
(wandering among trees)]; "He sauntered through
lovely, museful evenings in nature *nemorivagant*."

nephalist one who practises *nephalism* or complete
abstinence from the consumption of alcohol;
[very rare noun]; [synonym: *teetotaler*]

nephoscope an instrument for measuring the
velocity, direction, and altitude of clouds; [noun];
[Greek *néfos* cloud]

Neptune's kiss the unwelcome splash of water upon
one's backside whilst pooping; [noun]; [UK slang]

Neptunian pertaining to *Neptune,* Roman god of the sea; pertaining to the sea or ocean; [adj.]

Nergal god of death in Babylonian myth. – brandished a sword and a lion-headed mace; [Sumarian *Nergal* (lord of the big city)]

netherling clothing worn underneath other clothing; nethergarments; something or someone that inhabits the netherworld; [rare noun]

nethermind the subconscious mind; [rare noun]; "This is how he does it as a writer: he runs everything past his innocence, his *nethermind*, his first soul. He runs everything past his soul." – Martin Amis, *Experience: a Memoir*, 2001

nethers the genitals; [noun]; [UK slang]; [Luxembourgish *nidder* downwards]

netherworld a supposed location of post-death existence beneath the Earth's surface, esp. if a place of punishment; a hidden or sinister subculture; [noun]; [synonym: *underworld*]

neurodivergent possessing atypical neurology; [adj.]; [noun: *neurodiversity*]; [antonym: *neurotypical*]

New Great Game renewed geopolitical interest in the 21st c. from China, the United States, Russia and other countries in Central Asia largely due to the region's mineral wealth, esp. hydrocarbons; [the original *Great Game* was a 19th c. political & diplomatic competition between the Russian and British empires for influence and territory in Central Asia]

nexus a network; a connected group; the center of something; [noun]; [adj. *nexal*]; [Spanish & Portuguese *nexo* (connection, nexus)]

night-faring or **nightfaring** moving about or
traveling during the night; [archaic adj.];
[synonym: *nightwandering*]; "*nightfaring* creature"

nightscape a landscape at night or a depiction of
same; [noun]; "His verse painted a darkling scene
– a *nightscape* deep, mysterious, enchanting."

nimbostratus virga a type of *nimbostratus* cloud in
which precipitation evaporates before reaching
ground level; [noun]; [Latin *virga* (twig, rod, staff)]

nimiety state of being in excess; much more than is
necessary; [noun]; [synonym: *surfeit*]; [Spanish
nimio insignificant]; "There is a *nimiety*,
– a too-muchness – in all Germans."
– Samuel Taylor Coleridge, *Table Talk*, 1834

nirvana in Buddhism, a state of total freedom
from suffering – a blissful state of enlightened
experience; any state of paradise or of great
pleasure; [adj. *nirvanic*]; [Sanskrit *nirvāṇa* (blown
out, extinguished)]; "A clear sense of *nirvanic*
peace mantled the meadowed hills."

nivometric pertaining to the measuring of snowfall;
[adj.]; [Latin *nix* (snow, white hair)];
[Italian *nevometro* snow-gauge]

noble rot the beneficial form of *Botrytis cineria* –
a type of grey fungus that, if grapes infected
with it are picked under the right conditions
at the optimal time, can produce a very fine,
botrytized wine

nonchalance indifferent carelessness; a cool and
detached demeanor; [noun]; [adj. *nonchalant*];
[French *chaloir* (to heat, to matter)]

nondescript without distinguishing or easily
noticeable qualities or aspects; [adj.];
[synonym: *unexceptional*]

Nooksack Giant a tree in the American state of
Washington that supposedly measured 465 feet
(142m) high; arguably the world's tallest tree, it
produced 96,000 *board feet* of lumber when
felled in the 1890's

nook-shotten full of nooks and corners; [rare adj.];
[coined by William Shakespeare];
"...Norman bastards!
Mort de ma vie! If they march along
Unfought withal, but I will sell my dukedom,
To buy a slobbery and a dirty farm
In that *nook-shotten* isle of Albion."
– Shakespeare, *Henry V*, 1599

nostophobia fear of going back to one's home;
a fixed dislike or repugnant feeling toward
the past; [rare noun]; [antonym: *nostalgia*];
[Ancient Greek *nóstos* (a return home)]

nostrify or **nostrificate** to grant recognition of a
degree from a university in a foreign country;
to include something foreign as a part of one's
own culture; [verb]; [Italian *nostra* ours]

November Witch or **Witch of November** the high
winds common on the Great Lakes in autumn;
"The wind in the wires made a tattle-tale sound
And a wave broke over the railing
And every man knew, as the captain did too
T'was the *Witch of November* come stealin'"
– Gordon Lightfoot, *The Wreck of the Edmund
Fitzgerald*, 1976

novitiate a novice; a beginner; someone with limited knowledge or experience in a particular subject or pursuit; [noun]; [Greek *néos* (young, new)]

Nowhere Else a town in Tasmania, Australia

nth occurring at a very large but indefinite position in a series; [adj.]; [synonym: *umpteenth*]; "For the *nth* time..."

nugacious trifling; very insignificant or unimportant; [rare]; [synonym: *nugatory*]; "...things as *nugacious* as the colour of a habit, or the shape of a cowl." – Robert Southey, *Colloquy Part II...*, 1829

nullibiquitous not existing anywhere; [adj.]; [very rare & humorous]; [antonym: *ubiquitous*]

nulligravida a human female who has never become pregnant; [noun]; [Latin *gravis* heavy]

numerable finite; able to be numbered or counted; numerous; [adj.]; [antonym: *innumerable*]

O

obelus (pl. *obeli*) a dagger-like symbol used to indicate a footnote or other reference; [noun]

obequitate to ride around on a horse; to travel by horse; [rare verb]; [Latin *equitulus* (a young knight)]

oblivial pertaining to *oblivion* – a state of complete forgetfulness; [adj.]; "*oblivial* inebriation"

obmurmuration an act of complaining; [rare noun]; [Latin *obmurmurō* (I grumble)]

obsidian a type of glass produced by volcanoes; a black color with a slightly blue hue; describing something so colored; [noun & adj.]; [from *Obsidius*, an ancient Roman explorer who discovered *obsidian* or a similar stone in Ethiopia]

obvolvent curved downward; curved around something; [very rare adj.]

Ocean of Milk in Hindu cosmology, the fifth from the center of the seven oceans; the *devas* (deities) and *asuras* (demons) worked together for a millennium to churn this ocean and release a pitcher of *amrita*, the elixir of eternal life

octopodes a now rare plural form of octopus, considered by some more correct than *octopi*

oddling a person who is eccentric or very unusual; [rare noun]; [synonyms: *oddball* & *strangeling*]; "Her friends were *oddlings* all, some in mirrorshades, most ostentatiously artistic, and all engaged in creative, though often capricious, pursuits."

oddsboard the board showing the odds, esp. in sports gambling; [noun]

odium hatred; dislike; offensiveness; [noun]; [Italian *uggia* (moroseness, boredom)]

odorprint or **odourprint** a unique odor that may identify a person or a state of mind during which the odor was produced; [rare noun]; "Her *odorprint* eloquently expressed the stress of the day as he hugged her."

Odyssean of or relating to the Ancient Greek epic poem the *Odyssey* by Homer; characteristic of the epic's hero Odysseus or his voyages; [adj.]; "The journey took an *Odyssean* turn when they got lost and the car sh*t the bed."

Office Girls, The two prominent nunataks (rocky peaks protruding above a glacier) in Antarctica

Ogygian (oh-JIJ-ee-en) relating to *Ogyges*, a mythic king of ancient Greece, or to a great flood

during his reign; relating to the mythic Greek
isle *Ogygia*, home to the nymph Calypso;
primeval; very ancient and obscure; [rare adj.];
"Weary and wet the *Ogygian* shores I gain,
When the tenth sun descended to the main."
– Homer, the *Odyssey*, 7th c. BCE

Old World monkeys common name for the largest
primate family that includes 138 species

Oldenburg Horn, the a drinking horn of gilded
silver made for Christian I of Denmark in 1465 –
the horn now resides at Rosenborg Castle in
Copenhagen

omnicompetent capable of doing anything; very
competent in a wide variety of areas; [rare adj.];
[noun: *omnicompetence*]; "Her assistant was
as *omnicompetent* as a Wodehousian valet."

omnifarious extremely varied; of all possible
varieties; [adj.]; "the *omnifarious* life of a
tropical rainforest"

omnilucent casting light in all directions; all-
illuminating; [rare adj.]; [Portuguese *luzir*
(to shine)]; "*omnilucent* stars"

omnipatient very patient; able to endure many
hardships; [adj.]; "He was as *omnipatient* as Job."

onanistic relating to masturbation; in a way that
suggests masturbation – hence pointless, self-
congratulatory, etc.; [adj.]; [noun: *onanism*]; [the
biblical *Onan* "spilled his seed on the ground"];
"His *onanistic* award-acceptance speech
continued on and on *ad nauseam*."

ondoyant wavy, esp. used to describe art; having a
surface marked by waves; [rare adj.]; [French]

oneirogen something that creates or enhances a dreamlike state of consciousness; [rare noun]; [adj. *oneirogenic*]; "Always she was, for him, a species of *oneirogen* – he dreamt long, deep, and clear on nights after seeing her."

oneironaut one who explores or adventures in dream worlds, esp. through lucid dreaming; [rare noun]; [noun: *oneironautics*]; [Greek *óneiro* dream]

ooftish money; [archaic British slang]; [Yiddish]

oorie or **ourie** bleak; depressing; shivering due to cold; [rare adj.]; [Scotland]

orchidaceous relating to orchids; showy; ostentatious; [adj.]; [Greek *órchis* testicle]

Orion-Cygnus Arm or **Orion Bridge** the spiral arm of the Milky Way galaxy that contains the Solar System

Oropendolas or **Psarocolius** a genus of long-tailed, tropical birds at least partially bright yellow that live in large, communal hanging nests; [Spanish *oro* gold + *péndula* quill]

Ostrogoths a Roman-era Germanic people mostly occupying the Balkans; [adj. *Ostrogothic*]; [Proto-Germanic *austraz* eastern]

ostler a person employed to look after horses, esp. at an inn or stable; [noun]; [synonym: *groom*]

outercourse any sexual activity that does not include penetration; [rare noun]; [from *outer* + *intercourse*]

outgleam to shine more brightly; [rare verb]; "Venus *outgleams* even the most luminous star."

outlander an outsider; a foreigner; a stranger; [noun]; [synonyms: *outcomeling* & *strangeling*];

[German *Ausländer* foreigner]

outpassion to exceed in passion; [rare verb]

outsweeten to exceed in sweetness; [verb];
"When she wants to, she can *outsweeten*
grandma's apple pie."

overclass the upper class; the ruling class; [noun];
[synonym: *aristocracy*]

overmoist extremely moist; too moist; [rare adj.]

overpeopled too populated; overpopulated;
[rare adj.]; "*overpeopled* planets"

overponderous too heavy; too slow and ponderous;
[rare adj.]

overquell to quell or subdue completely; to gain
power over; [rare verb]

oversoul the spiritual unity of all being; the all-
containing soul; [noun]; "...that Unity, that *Over-
soul*, within which every man's particular being is
contained and made one with all other..."
– Ralph Waldo Emerson, *The Over-Soul*, 1841

overveil to cover; to veil; to spread over; [verb]

overview effect the cognitive shift experienced by
some astronauts after viewing Earth from space –
often includes overwhelming emotions, a deeper
perception of Earth's fragile beauty, and a greater
sense of connection with humanity; [noun]

owleries places owls live or frequent; owl homes;
[noun]; "England, once the land of heroes, is itself
sunk now to a dim *owlery*, and habitation of
doleful creatures, intent only on money-making
and other forms of catching mice..."
– Thomas Carlyle, *No. III Downing Street*, 1850

owly-eyed having good night vision; wide-eyed
from fear or shock; [rare adj.]

oxblood a dark, brownish-red color; describing
something so colored; [noun & adj.]

oxishly done in the manner of an ox; in an ox-like
way; [rare adverb]; "staring *oxishly*"

P

Pachamama an Earth Mother type goddess –
mother of moon goddess *Mama Killa*;
[Incan myth.]; [Quechua languages, literally:
World Mother]

Pacific spiny lumpsucker a globular, bony fish only
about two inches long – endemic to the north
Pacific Ocean

Page 99 test reading a book of fiction's 99th
page before deciding to read or purchase it;
[suggested by 20th c. English novelist & literary
critic Ford Madox Ford (1873-1939)]

palatine uvula (pl. *palatine uvulae*) the fleshy
appendage that hangs from the back of the
mouth – only found in humans; [noun];
[Latin *ūvula* (little grape)]

pallid appearing weak or pale; [adj.]; [synonym:
ghastly]; [Italian *pallido* (pale, bleak)]; "The
four-month Arctic night left him *pallid* and frail."

pancosmic throughout the universe; [rare adj.];
"a *pancosmic* intelligence"

Pandurica an ancient castle in Montenegro

pangless painless; without a pang; without sudden
agony; [adj.]

panjandrum an important person; a self-important
person; [nonce word coined by 18th British
dramatist Samuel Foote]

panniculus (pl. *panniculi*) excess fatty tissue in the lower abdominal region; "The beach was lousy with hairy, shirtless old men – their *panniculi* bobbing as they strode, much too confidently."

panpsychism the theory that all matter has a mental origin; [noun]; [French *psychique* psychic]

Panslavonian or **Panslavic** pertaining to all Slavic peoples or languages; "*Panslavic* mythologies"

Panthalassa or **Panthalassic Ocean** the superocean that surrounded the supercontinent *Pangaea* – it covered almost 70% of Earth's surface 250 million years BCE; [Ancient Greek *pan-* (all) + *thálassa* (sea)]

pantherine panther-like, esp. in color; [adj.]; [synonym: *pardine*]; "her *pantherine* stride"

pantropical widespread in Earth's tropical areas; [adj.]; [biology]; "a *pantropical* distribution"

parachronic existing in a separate timeline; pertaining to a connection between temporal dimensions; [adj.]; "*parachronic* lives"

paradigm (pl. *paradigmata*) a pattern or model for a way of doing something; a pattern of thinking; a system of beliefs; [noun]; [adj. *paradigmatic*]; [Greek *parádeigma* example]

paradisian of, like, or relating to a paradise; delightful; heavenly; [adj.]; [synonyms: *paradisal* & *paradisiac*]; "*paradisian* isles"

paragram a pun; a play on words; [noun]

parahippocampal gyrus (pl. *parahippocampal gyri*) area of the brain important for retrieving from, and encoding into, memory the images of places such as landscapes or cityscapes; [noun]

parallelless without equal; matchless; peerless; [rare adj.]; "The belvedere offered *parallelless*

views of the grassy swards, cascading down
to a tumultuous sea."

paramour an illicit male or female lover;
[archaic noun]

paranormal romance a subgenre of romantic fiction
and speculative fiction that focuses on romance,
but includes elements from fantasy & science
fiction, such as time travel, paranormal or alien
settings, psychic abilities, fantastic creatures, etc.

paranormality the quality of being supernatural;
a state of supposed reality where ghosts, spirits,
and abilities like telepathy exist; [noun];
"The murky alleyways and umbratic netherworlds
of *paranormality* were the fallen prophet's favored
haunts."

parapet a low wall; a low wall on a roof, often
designed for safety; a wall used as a military
fortification; [noun]; [synonym: *breastwork*];
[Italian *petto* chest]

paraphiliac in sexology, one who suffers from
paraphilia, the abnormal and often extreme
sexual attraction to things or situations that
are not normally of a sexual nature; [noun];
[very rare antonym: *normophile*]

parazonium (pl. *parazonia*) a ceremonial dagger,
long and triangular, of ancient Rome; [noun]

paregmenon (pl. *paregmena*) the pairing of cognates
(words with common derivations) to achieve
some effect; "*Sense and Sensibility* is an 1811
novel by Jane Austen"

pareidolia (pair-eye-DOE-lia) when humans impose
a meaningful interpretation upon random stimuli,
usually visual; [noun]; [rare adj. *pareidolic*];

[example: *seeing animal shapes in clouds*];
[Ancient Greek *pará* (beside) + *eídōlon* (phantom, image)]

parergon (pl. *parerga*) a piece of work that is supplementary or a by-product of a larger or more important work; "...the running and control of double agents is an ... infinitely complicated task. It could not be done as a *parergon* by any intelligence department elsewhere..."
– J. C. Masterman, *The Double-Cross System*, 1945

Pareto principle a proposition stating that for most outcomes, roughly 80% of consequences result from 20% of causes; [20th c. Italian polymath Vilfredo *Pareto* observed that 80% of Italy's land was owned by 20% of the population]

parfay by my faith; verily; [obsolete interjection]

parliament collective term for a group of owls

peacocking showing off like a peacock; [verb]; [synonym: *showboating*]

Pegasus a winged-horse that sprung from the blood of Medusa, created the fountain of the Muses with a blow of his hoof, and helped Bellerophon defeat the Chimaera; also a constellation prominent in the northern, evening sky in autumn; [adj. *Pegasean*]; [Greek myth.]

Peninsular Spanish the standard form of the Spanish language in use on the Iberian Peninsula; [noun]; [synonym: *Castilian Spanish*]

Penrose stairs or **impossible staircase** a 2-dimensionally depicted loop of stairs that appear to endlessly ascend or descend in an impossible fashion; a reoccurring theme in the work of Dutch artist M. C. Escher; [Sir Roger *Penrose*, 20th English mathematician]

penultimatum in diplomacy, a demand for certain terms of an agreement expressed as an ultimatum in hopes of compelling acceptance, but then superseded by more negotiation instead of final consequences; [noun]; [Latin *paene* almost + *ultimus* final]

peragrate to travel over or through; [obsolete verb]

perchance maybe; perhaps; by chance; [archaic adverb]; [archaic synonym: *peradventure*]; "And now I'm in the world alone, Upon the wide, wide sea; But why should I for others groan, When none will sigh for me? *Perchance* my Dog will whine in vain, Till fed by stranger hands; But long ere I come back again He'd tear me where he stands." – Lord Byron, *Childe Harold's Pilgrimage*, 1812

percheron a draught horse breed; [*Perche*, formerly a French district]

percurrent in biology, running throughout; running the whole length; [adj.]; "*percurrent* veins"

Perfidious Albion a mostly historical, derogatory term representing the UK as treacherous and deceptive in international affairs; [poetic]; [*perfidious* (disloyal) + *Albion* (an old name for England)]; "*Perfidious Albion* yielded up all her French colonial conquests, except Mauritius, Tobago, and St. Lucia." – John H. Rose, *The Life of Napolean I*, 1901

performative being done as a performance to create an impression of how one wants to be seen by others; relating to a performance of an artistic nature; [adj.]; *"performative tears"*

perinarial surrounding a nostril; [very rare adj.]

perineal raphe the visible ridge of tissue on humans running between the sphincter and the sexual organs; [noun]; [Italian *rafe* suture]

peripersonal space the space around an individual within reach of an arm or a leg; [noun]

peri-urban neighboring an urban area; situated between suburbs and countryside; [adj.]; *"a peri-urban hamlet"*

perlucidus *altocumulus* or *stratocumulus* clouds with small gaps; [noun]; [Latin *perlucidus* (transparent, pellucid)]

person from Porlock someone who interrupts or intrudes, preventing the completion of something very important, esp. an artistic endeavor; [very rare noun]; [adj. *Porlockian*]; [a *person from Porlock* infamously interrupted Coleridge while he was composing *Kubla Khan*, preventing the poem's completion]

perulate in botany, having *perulae*, or the scales of a leaf bud; [adj.]

petrescent petrifying; converting into stone; [adj.]; [Italian *pietra* stone]

Peutinger Table an ancient map depicting the Roman road network in parts of Europe, Asia, and North Africa; [noun]; [Konrad *Peutinger* 16th c. German archaeologist]

phallocentric male focused; centered upon the *phallus*; [adj.]; [Ancient Greek *phallós* penis]

phantastica collective term for hallucinogenic drugs; [very rare noun]; [Italian *fantastica* imaginary]; [coined by German pharmacologist Louis Lewin in 1928]

phantom settlement or **paper town** a town that appears on a map but doesn't actually exist – included by accident or placed purposefully by the map's publisher as a *copyright trap*; [noun]

pharaonic like or pertaining to a *pharaoh*; tyrannical; notably large or luxurious; [adj.]

phasma (pl. *phasmata*) an apparition; a phantom; [rare noun]; [Latin *phasma* phantom]

phedinkus nonsense; malarkey; [very rare noun]; [coined in 1935 by American short-story writer Damon Runyon]

philonoetic intellectual; loving intellectual activities; [very rare adj.]; [Ancient Greek *phílos* loving + *noētikós* intellectual]

philotherian a person with a strong love for animals, esp. if loving many different species; [very rare noun]; [Greek *thirío* beast]

phthartic deadly, esp. used to describe something poisonous; destructive; [obsolete adj.]; [Greek *phthartikos* destructive]

piggery a place where pigs are bred or kept; pig-like behavior; [noun]; "Your innate *piggery* was on full display at the buffet."

pigman (pl. *pigmen*) a male farm worker that feeds and otherwise tends to pigs

pignorative pledging; pawning; describing something secured by a solemn promise or a deposit; [rare adj.]; [noun: *pignoration*]; "a *pignorative* contract"

Pigovian tax a government tax on any negative externality caused by a given market activity; [example: *the tax on a factory polluting the environment*]; [antonym: *Pigovian subsidy*]; [Arthur Cecil *Pigou*, 20th c. English economist]

pigsney or **pigsny** darling; an old term of endearment; [England]; [obsolete]

piliferous having or growing hair; [adj.]; [Italian, Spanish & Portuguese *pelo* hair]; "a most *piliferous* young man"

Pillars of Creation dramatic, elongated clouds of interstellar gas and dust in the Eagle Nebula from which new stars are slowly being born – about 7000 light years from Earth; [astronomy]

Pillars of Hercules the ancient name for the promontories that mark the western limit of the Mediterranean world: the *Rock of Gibraltar* and *Jebel Musa* in Morocco

pineclad covered in pine trees; [adj.]; [poetic & rare]; "...then the moon... appeared behind the jagged crest of a beetling, *pineclad* rock, and by its light I saw around us a ring of wolves..." – Bram Stoker, Dracula, 1897

pinguescent becoming fat or overweight; flourishing; [adj.]; [archaic & rare]; [Latin *pinguēscō* (I grow fat or rich)]

pink fairy armadillo the smallest species of armadillo with silky, yellowish-white fur – endemic to arid regions of central Argentina

piratical plundering; predatory; relating to or similar to pirates; [adj.]; [Ancient Greek *peîra* (experiment, attempt)]; "Our prices will be

predacious, *piratical*, prohibitive, and profitable."
– Marie Oemler, *A Woman Named Smith*, 1919

piscifauna the fish life of a region; [noun];
[Romanian *peşte* fish]

placentious pleasing; amiable; [obsolete adj.]

plateaux a plural form of plateau; "In the mountains
I used to flee the deep valleys for the passes and
plateaux; at the very least, I was a man of the
uplands." – Albert Camus, *The Chute*, 1956

pleasing fungus beetles a family of beetles with
over 100 genera; [*pleasing* because they have
large and colorful patterns and *fungus* because
they feed upon it]

plenilune the full moon; [poetic]; [adj. *plenilunary*];
[antonym: *new moon*]; [Latin *plēnus* full];
"Another Cynthia, and another queen,
Whose glory, like a lasting *plenilune*,
Seems ignorant of what it is to wane."
– Ben Jonson, *The Fountain of Self-Love*, 1601

plexus (pl. *plexi*) in anatomy, a network of nerves and
blood vessels; an interwoven combination of
elements in a system; a network; [noun];
"I am a *plexus* of weaknesses, an impotent Prince,
a doubtful gentleman."
– Robert Louis Stevenson, *Prince Otto*, 1885

plumeless without feathers or plumes; devoid of
plumage; [adj.]; [Lithuanian *plùnksna* feather];
"...like eagles, his thoughts were first callow; yet,
born *plumeless*, they came to soar." – Herman
Melville, *Mardi: And a Voyage Thither*, 1864

plutocrat one who holds power mainly because
of riches; someone whose wealth gives him
or her power or influence; [adj. *plutocratic*];

[Ancient Greek *ploûtos* wealth + *krátos* power];
"...a *plutocratic* and corrupt political system."

pluvial relating to rain; rainy; produced by rain;
[synonyms: *pluvious & pluviose*]; [Latin *pluvia*
rain]; "*pluvial* clouds"

pneumatic pertaining to gases, esp. air; powered
by compressed air; in zoology, having air-filled
cavities, such as in bones; spiritual, or related to
the soul; curvaceous, full-breasted, or bouncy;
[adj.]; [Greek *pnévma* (soul, spirit, intellect)];
[last def. very rare – used by Aldous Huxley
in *Brave New World*, 1932]

pococurante apathetic; indifferent; a person that
embodies those traits; [adj. & noun]; [synonyms:
nonchalant, disinterested]; [from Senator
Pococurante in Voltaire's *Candide*, 1759];
[Italian *poco* little + *curante* caring]

podex (pl. *podices*) in anatomy, rectum or fundament;
[noun]; [Latin]

Point Nemo or **the oceanic pole of inaccessibility**
the point on Earth farthest from land – in the
South Pacific, 1670 miles equidistant from three
islands; [named for Captain *Nemo* in the 1869
Jules Verne novel *20,000 Leagues Under the Sea*]

Polaris Australis or **Sigma Octantis** the pole star of
the southern hemisphere that is only one degree
from the *south celestial pole* – much fainter than
the North Star, so not often used for navigation;
the dimmest star to be represented on a national
flag (Brazil)

polyphagia an extraordinarily large appetite for
food; [noun]; [adj. *polyphagic*]; [synonym:
hyperphagia]; [Ancient Greek *éphagon* devour]

ponderosity something that requires a great deal of thought; heaviness; [noun]; "Her thesis was fraught with philosophical *ponderosities*."

Porphyrios a large whale that for over 50 years attacked ships near Constantinople in 6th c. CE, only to eventually beach itself near the mouth of the Black Sea; [possibly named after the giant *Porphyrion* who fought the gods in Greek myth.]

portend to act as an omen or a warning; to signify; to denote; [verb]; [adj. *portentive* & *portentous*]; [synonym: *augur*]; "The young ambassador's many gaucheries did not *portend* détente."

portmanteau (pl. *portmanteaux*) a large, leather travelling case; a word created by combining two or more words; describing that type of word; [noun & adj.]; [Spanish *manto* (shroud, cloak)]; "A good *portmanteau* word is interesting or useful without being too ponderous or lengthy."

postbellum or **post-bellum** of a period of time following a war, esp. the American Civil War; [adj.]; [Latin *bellum* war]; "the *postbellum* South"

postdiluvian after a flood, esp. after the Biblical Flood; after something as disasterous as a flood; [adj.]; [synonym: *postdiluvial*]

prajnaparamita a perfected way of seeing the true nature of reality; transcendental knowledge in Theravāda Bhuddism; [Sanskrit *prajñā* wisdom + *pāramitā* transcendent]

preadamite an inhabitant of Earth that lived before the Biblical Adam; a person that believes humankind existed before Adam; [noun]; [adj. *preadamic*]; "*preadamic* theories"

precipitous very steep; like a precipice; hasty or rash; sudden; [adj.]; "Gazing down the *precipitous* slope left her vertiginous."

Pre-Code Hollywood the period in American film history that started shortly before widespread adoption of sound in 1929 and ended after the enforcement of the Hays Code (censorship guidelines) in mid-1934; some films made during this time included interracial relationships, sexual innuendo, intense violence, profanity, drug use, homosexuality, *et alia*; [historical]

primacy the state of being the best or the first in time, rank, power, etc.; "the *primacy* of our clan"

primal scene in psychoanalysis, the first time a child sees (or visualizes) his or her parents having sex; [coined by Sigmund Freud in 1914 – German *Urszene*]; "The *primal scene* is the site at which the issues of ego differentiation become translated into the issues of the Oedipus complex." – W. Kerrigan, *The Sacred Complex*, 1983

primeval belonging to the earliest times; having existed since the first ages; in an original state; primitive; [adj.]; [Latin *primus* first + *aevum* age]; "This is the forest *primeval*. The murmuring pines and the hemlocks, / Bearded with moss, and in garment green, indistinct in the twilight, / Stand like Druids of eld, with voices sad and prophetic..." – Henry Wadsworth Longfellow, *Evangeline*, 1847

prismatic relating to a prism; having varied or brilliant colors; [adj.]; [synonym: *polychromatic*]; "The morning rose glorious and *prismatic*: dew-moistened meadows and sunshot wood beneath a severe clear sky."

private revelation an instance of revelation of divine reality to a person or group, rather than to the public at large; [antonym: *public revelation*]; [Christian theology]

prolate spheroid a shape defined by an ellipse rotated around its major axis (its longest diameter); [noun]; "Rugby balls are *prolate spheroids*, while American footballs are too pointy to be true *prolate spheroids*."

Prometheus an almost 5000-year-old bristlecone pine tree in eastern Nevada that was cut down for research purposes in 1964; [named for the figure in Greek myth. that stole fire from the Olympian gods and give it to humankind]

prosaic overly plain or simple; boring; relating to or similar to prose; [adj.]; [synonym: *unimaginative*]

Proserpina or **Proserpine** an ancient Roman goddess and queen of the underworld – nearly equivalent to the Greek goddess *Persephone*

protean variable; easily able to change forms; [adj.]; [synonym: *polymorphic*]; [in Greek myth., *Proteus* was a sea god that could shapeshift]

protofascist or **proto-fascist** in politics, espousing opinions and policies that tend toward or parrot fascism; describing a political system that is showing the beginnings of fascism; an individual that holds such opinions or is part of such a political system; [adj. & noun]

protohuman relating to early humans or the beginnings of humankind; a member of one of the earliest human species that preceded *Homo sapiens*; [adj. & noun]; [Greek *prôtos* first]

protuberant swelling; bulging out; [adj.]; [noun: *protuberance*]; [verb: *protuberate*]

provenance the place of origin; the source; in art, a piece's ownership history; [noun]; [rare adj. *provenantial*]; [French *provenance* origin]; "of unknown *provenance*"

proventriculus the first part of a bird's stomach wherein digestive enzymes mix with food in this rod-shaped organ before heading to the gizzard; [noun]; [Spanish *vientre* (abdomen, belly)]

psammophile (SAM-o-file) an organism that thrives in sand; [noun]; [adj. *psammophilous*]; [synonym: *arenophile*]

psychobilly a genre of rock music that combines elements of *rockabilly* and *punk rock* – popular in Europe in the 1980s

psychogeography the scientific study of the effect factors related to geography have on human behavior or psychological disposition; [adj. *psychogeographic*]; "*psychogeographic* depression is not uncommon in pluvial climes"

psychonaut someone that explores his or her own psyche, esp. by using psychedelic drugs or otherwise altering their state of consciousness; [synonym: *neuronaut*]; [Ancient Greek *psychē* (soul, spirit) and *naútēs* (sailor)]

puerility the state or quality of being childish; that which is childish; [noun]; [adj. *puerile*]; [Latin *puer* boy]; "Your *puerilities* are an overflowing fount of near-constant embarrassment."

puerperium (pl. *puerperia*) in obstetrics, the month or so after childbirth during which the mother's uterus returns to a *prepartum* state; [noun]

puerperous (pwair-per-ous) bearing children; [rare adj.]

pulchrify to make beautiful; to beautify; [rare verb]; [noun: *pulchritude*]

Punta Tempesta a mountain in the Cottian Alps of Italy

pupation the act or process of an insect (in *pupa* form) developing from larva to adult; [noun]; [verb: *pupate*]; [Latin *pūpa* (girl, puppet, pupa)]

purl to make a murmuring sound, as flowing water; an eddy or ripple in flowing fluid; [verb & noun]; [Old Norse *purla* (to babble)]; "...the *purling* rill" – Alexander Pope, *An Essay on Man*, 1734

Purple Forbidden Enclosure, the in ancient Chinese astrology, a large constellation divided into 39 groups and totaling 163 stars

purple fringeless orchid an orchid species native to moist forests in eastern America, including areas of the Ozark Mountains – produces purple flowers in summer

purseproud or **purse-proud** having an air of superiority regarding the possession of riches; [adj.]; "New money is more *purseproud* than old."

Pyrenean relating to the Pyrenees, the mountain range dividing France and Spain; someone from or living in the Pyrenees; [adj. & noun]; [Ancient Greek *pūrén* (fruit-stone)]; "*Pyrenean* hospitality"

Pythonesque of humor, absurd, zany, or ludicrously surreal; [adj.]; [British comedy troupe Monty *Python*]; "*Pythonesque* skits"

Q

quafftide the time or season for consuming alcoholic drinks; [noun]; [archaic & rare]; [Old Irish *cuách* (cup, goblet)]

quagmire an area of swampy or wet ground; figuratively, a troubled and tangled up situation; [noun]; [adj. *quaggy*]; [synonym: *mireland*]; [Swedish & Norwegian *myr* (moor, marsh)]

quasicrystalline describing something that has a structure similar to a crystal; [rare adj.]

quasiperiodic nearly periodic; repeating at irregular intervals; [rare adj.]; [noun: *quasiperiodicity*]; [Italian *quasi* almost]

quaver to shake in a quivering or trembling manner; to speak or sing in a trembling way; an instance of same; [verb & noun]; "her voice *quavered* with emotion"

queencraft the skills needed to fulfill the part of queen in a monarchical government or in a royal family; [noun]; [masculine: *kingcraft*]; "Her combined skills of *queencraft* & bitchcraft were quite formidable."

quenchless describing that which cannot be quenched; unable to satisfy a literal or figurative thirst; [adj.]; [synonym: *insatiable*]; [Middle English *quenchen* (to fulfill one's desire)]; "His thirst for power & riches seemed *quenchless*."

querken or **querk** to grunt or moan; [verb]; [Old Norse *kvirkja* (to strangle)]

quickbeam a rowan tree, AKA *mountain ash*; endemic to cool temperate regions of the

Northern Hemisphere; [noun]; [Old English *cwicbēam* (living tree)]

quicksilver the metal mercury; unpredictable; mercurial; [noun & adj.]

quill pig porcupine; [archaic]; "A single meeting may cure a dog of his curiosity regarding *quill pigs*."

quintessence in physics, a hypothetical form of dark energy that explains the increasing acceleration of the universe's expansion; [from *quinta essentia* – Latin for *fifth element*, the first four being *baryons, neutrinos, dark matter*, and *radiation*]

quisling a traitor; one who collaborates with an enemy; [noun]; [verb: *quisle*]; [military officer Vidkun *Quisling* – head of the Nazi collaborationist government of Norway during World War Two]

R

railbird a gambler, esp. one who bets at horse racetracks; [noun]; [American slang]

Rainbow Serpent a creator deity in Aboriginal Australian myth.

rainbows and unicorns (pl. only) a wonderful scenario, esp. if also unrealistic; [synonym: *sunshine & rainbows*]; [antonym: *doom & gloom*]

rainshadow an area of unusual aridity due to nearby geographic landforms, often mountain ranges

rambutan the fruit of the *rambutan* tree (*nephelium lappaceum*) native to SE Asia; [noun]; [Malay]

Rampjaar the year 1672, when France nearly conquered the Dutch Republic; [noun]; [Dutch *Disaster Year*]; [historical]

rancescent becoming rancid or sour; [adj.]; [Latin *rancida* stinking]; "*rancescent* milks"

rarefy or **rarify** to make rare; to make thinner, more porous, or less dense; [verb]; [adj. *rarified*]

Rastaban or **Beta Draconis A** the primary star in a binary star system 380 light years distant in the constellation Draco; [Arabic *ra's ath-thu'ban* (head of the dragon)]

rat-arsed very drunk; [rare adj.]; [UK slang]; "After umpteen pints, my mate was so *rat-arsed* I felt it prudent to walk him home."

Ravenser Odd or **Ravensrodd** a port town in NE England destroyed by *Saint Marcellus's flood* in 1362; [Old Norse *hrafn's eyr* (raven's tongue)]

rawk a thick, dreary fog or mist; [rare noun]; [adj. *rawky*]; [UK]; [Swedish *rök* smoke]; "And here are nameless flowers, Culled in cold and *rawky* hours..." – John Clare, 19th c. English poet

razorable fit to be shaved; [very rare adj.]; [coined by Shakespeare in *The Tempest*, 1623]; "A week later he emerged from the forest gaunt and *razorable*."

reality tunnel the theory that each individual interprets the world differently due to a unique, unconscious set of mental filters formed from beliefs and experiences; [noun]; [coined by 20th c. American psychologist Timothy Leary]

rectosigmoid in anatomy, of the *rectum* and the *sigmoid colon*; [adj.]; "the *rectosigmoid* junction"

Red Queen hypothesis the theory that a given species must evolve or go extinct; [coined by Leigh Van Valen, 20th c. American evolutionary biologist; in *Alice in Wonderland*, the *Red Queen* tells Alice she has to keep running to stay in the same place]

red squill a flowering plant that grows from a large bulb – common in rocky coastal habitat of the Mediterranean Basin; [noun]

Red Thread of Fate an east Asian belief, originating from Chinese myth., that a red thread connects two people that are destined to meet in the future and enjoy their true love together

red tree brain fungus common name for *peniophora rufa*, a species of crust fungus that grows on the bark of dead aspen trees in northern and mountainous areas of North America; [noun]

redolent fragrant; sweet-smelling; reminiscent; [adj.]; [noun: *redolence*]; [synonym: *aromatic*]; [Latin *redoleō* (I emit a scent)];
"...in the country... the fine old trees, *redolent* of earth's loveliest mythology, when the dryades peopled their green shadows;"
– Letitia Elizabeth Landon, *Francesca Carrara*, 1834

refraction in physics, the bending or change of direction resulting from a wave moving from one medium to another, as light from air to water; [noun]; [adj. *refractive*]

rejuvenescent becoming young again; describing that which causes a return to youth or any of its attributes; [adj.]; [verb: *rejuvenate*]; [antonym: *senescent*]

relumine or **relume** to light or illuminate anew; to rekindle; [rare verb]; [Esperanto *lumo* light];
"Then I bethought me of the glorious doom

Of those who sternly struggle to *relume*
The lamp of Hope o'er man's bewildered lot;"
– Percy Bysshe Shelley, *The Revolt of Islam*, 1817

remontado someone who returns to the hills, mountains, deep forest, or other remote area after living in civilization for a while; [very rare noun]; [Spanish, literally: *re-mounted*]

remunerable that may be rewarded; fit or proper to be recompensed; [adj.]; [verb: *remunerate*]; "an honorable and *remunerable* vocation"

renascent rising into being again; being reborn; [adj.]; [Esperanto *naski* (to give birth)]; "The hours, days, and weeks fled by, filled with *renascent* joys."
– Honoré De Balzac, *The Lily of the Valley*, 1835

renegado a renegade; a rebel; [archaic noun]; [Spanish]

repletion superabundant fullness; the state of being completely full; [noun]; [adj. *replete*]; "The provender was not of high quality, yet his hunger so extreme that soon he feasted beyond *repletion*."

requiem a religious ceremony to honor a dead person, esp. in Catholicism; a musical composition accompanying such a ceremony; music honoring the dead; [noun]; [synonym: *threnody*]; [Latin *per quiētem* (in a dream)]; "To cease upon the midnight with no pain, While thou art pouring forth thy soul abroad In such an ecstasy! Still wouldst thou sing, and I have ears in vain – To thy high *requiem* become a sod."
– John Keats, *Ode to a Nightingale*, 1819

resomation a process that dissolves a corpse in a chemical compound at high temperature and pressure; [rare noun]; [Greek *sóma* body]

retiarius (pl. *retiari* or *retiarii*) in ancient Rome, a type of gladiator whose main weapon is a casting net; [noun]; [Italian *rete* net]; [historical]

retroflex bent, curved, or turned backwards, esp. sharply; [adj.]; [noun: *retroflexion*]; "The tree was notable for several curiously *retroflex* branches."

revolutionaire a revolutionary or revolutionist; a person who revolts, esp. against a repressive government; [rare noun]; [French]

rhapsodic very emotional; rapturous; pertaining to a *rhapsody* – an overly enthusiastic or exulted expression of feeling; [adj.]; [verb: *rhapsodize*]; "In passionate moments there was the unfamiliar, poetic, *rhapsodic* in his utterance which turned the world into a corner of heaven." – William J. Locke, *Where Love Is*, 1903

ridibund easy to laugh; generally happy; [rare adj.]; [Sicilian *rìdiri* (to laugh)]

Rimbaudian relating to, or in the style of, 19th c. French poet Arthur *Rimbaud*, known for his surreal themes and for representing absolute truths symbolically; [adj.]

rindle a small watercourse or gutter; [noun]

ringpiece the human anus, sphincter, or less commonly, rectum; [rare noun]; [UK slang]

Riphean Mountains a mountain range supposed by ancient Greco-Roman geographers to be in the far north of Eurasia and the source of *Boreas* – the North Wind; [from the Ancient Greek word for a *wind gust*]

ripsnorter a wildly energetic or loud, outspoken person; an event that was extreme in some way; [noun]; [American slang]; [synonym: *humdinger*]

rizzler a cool, good person; a charismatic person; [noun]; [American slang]; [from *rizz* – short for charisma]

robinsonade a genre of adventure fiction wherein the main character is stranded on an island and has to use his or her wits to survive; [noun]; [*Robinson* Crusoe, the titular hero of Daniel Defoe's 1715 novel]

Rock Apes of Gibraltar *Barbary macaques* inhabiting the Gibraltar Nature Reserve and originally imported from Morocco – now the only wild monkey population in Europe

rodentia an order of mammals having large incisor teeth – incl. mice, marmots, beavers, and 40% of all mammal species; [Latin *rōdēns* gnawing]

rodomontade vain boasting; the act of boasting to impress others; pretentiously boastful; [noun & adj.]; [from *Rodomonte*, a boastful character in Matteo Boiardo's 1483 epic poem *Orlando Innamorato*]

roman à clef a novel about real events, but overlaid with a veneer of fiction with made-up names representing real people; [French, literally: *novel with a key*]

Romantic chess a style of chess popular in the 18ᵗʰ c. that emphasized swift, tactical movements rather than long-term strategic planning and prioritized winning with style over simply winning

roofscape a landscape or viewscape in which the roofs of buildings dominate; [noun]; "His paintings of European *roofscapes*..."

rorid or **roscid** dewy; bedewed; [very rare adj.]; [synonym: *rorulent*]; [Latin *rōs* dew]

rosarium (pl. *rosaria*) a rose garden; [Spanish & Italian *rosa* rose]; "The property was exquisitely landscaped and included several *rosaria*."

roughcast a crude model; a rough surface, like stucco walls; unpolished; to shape crudely; [noun, adj. & verb]

ruinous causing ruin; calamitous, esp. in a financial context; [adj.]; [noun: *ruinousness*]

rump state a country or state that is a remnant of a much larger state that was broken up by annexation, revolution, secession, etc.; [noun]

rumpalicious having a shapely and attractive bum; [adj.]; [American slang]; [synonym: *callipygian*]

runecraft knowledge of runes or of deciphering runic characters; skill in the use of runes for magical purposes; [noun]

rupestrine living or growing on or among rocks; [adj.]; [synonyms: *rupicolous* & *rupicoline*]; [Latin *rūpes* rock]; [Italian *rupi* (rocky cliffs)]

Ruritanian having the characteristics of most romantic fiction, such as adventure and romance; describing a fictitious or hypothetical foreign government; [adj.]; [*Ruritania,* a fictional kingdom in works by 20th c. British novelist Anthony Hope]; "*Ruritanian* romance is a genre of literature, film, and theatre set in a fictional country, often in Central or Eastern Europe."

S

Sabians a mysterious religious group mentioned thrice in the Quran

sacroiliac relating to the *sacrum* and *ilium* bones or to the lower back area; [adj.]; [synonym: *iliosacral*]

saffron an orange-yellow color, like the color of a lion; a valuable spice; having an orange-yellow color; [noun & adj.]

Sahelian kingdoms a series of empires that ruled the *Sahel* – the grasslands spanning Africa south of the Sahara – from the 8th to the 19th century; these kingdoms could not expand further south because the camels and horses they relied upon were unsuited to forest travel and susceptible to the region's diseases; [historical]

Saint Elmo's fire or **Witchfire** an electrical discharge, or *corona*, seen around a rod-like object (such as a mast, spire, or chimney) that is caused by ionization of the atmosphere during certain weather conditions; [noun]; [Saint Erasmus of Formia (AKA *St. Elmo*) – patron saint of sailors]

salamandrine relating to or like a salamander; resistant or impervious to fire; [adj.]; [first def. synonym: *salamandroid*]; [second def. is from legendary salamanders being ascribed an affinity with fire by some ancient writers]

salivant something, esp. a drug, that causes salivation; producing salivation; [noun & adj.]; [synonym: *sialogogue*]; [Ancient Greek *síalon* saliva]

Samudra manthan a major episode in Hindu lore that explains the origin of *amrita*, the elixir of eternal life; [Sanskrit, literally: *churning of the ocean of milk*]

sandscape a landscape dominated by sand, esp. beach or sand dunes; [noun]

sandspout sand that is lifted and funnelled into a spout shape by a whirlwind; [rare noun]; [synonym: *sand column*]

sapiosexual sexually drawn to mental abilities more than physical attractiveness; a *sapiosexual* person; [adj. & noun]; [rare]; [2nd def. synonym: *sapiophile*]; [Spanish & Portuguese *sapiente* wise]

saprotrophic relating to an organism that feeds on decaying organic material; [rare adj.]; [noun: *saprotroph*]; [Ancient Greek *saprós* (rotten, putrid)]

sarcastic fringehead a small, hardy, usually brown fish with aggressive behaviors – endemic to the Pacific Ocean

sardoodledom finely crafted works of drama that have insignificant plots; [rare noun]; [19th c. French dramatist Victorien *Sardou* + *doodle* + *-dom*; coined in 1895 by George Bernard Shaw in reference to Sardou's plays]

satiety the state of being pleasantly satisfied or satiated; [noun]; [antonym: *famishment*]; "Thou lovest: but ne'er knew love's sad *satiety*." – Percy Bysshe Shelley, *To a Skylark*, 1820

savoir-faire the ability to act and speak appropriately to the occasion; [noun]; [French *savoir-faire* (know-how)]; "His wit and natural *savoir-faire* made him a beloved guest at gatherings both formal and loose."

scamander to wander with no definite purpose; [verb]; [archaic & very rare]; [likely from

Scamander, an old name for the Turkish river
Karamenderes]

scaturient gushing forth; effusive; overflowing;
[rare adj.]; [noun: *scaturience*]; [Italian *scaturìre*
(to flow from)]; "This play is the shimmering
scaturience of an intelligence and a sensibility of
the very first distinction."
– Edmund Wilson, *Shores of Light,* 1985

scialytic (sigh-uh-lit-ic) dispelling or removing
shadows; [very rare adj.]; [Ancient Greek *skiá*
shadow + *lúsis* loosening]; "*scialytic* sunbeams"

sciamachy shadow-boxing; fighting that is make-
believe or doomed to be unsuccessful; [noun];
[Greek *skiá* shadow]

scobberlotcher an idler or layabout; [rare noun]

Scotch mist a particularly cold and thick mist; a light
rain that obscures visibility; a thing that is very
hard to find or may not even exist; [noun]; [UK]

Scouser someone from Liverpool, England;
a Liverpudlian; [noun]; [*scouse* – a common
stew in Liverpool]

Scouserati notable people from Liverpool, England;
[UK]; [rare noun]

scrivener a person employed as a writer or to draft
contracts, prepare letters, etc.; [archaic noun];
[synonym: *scribe*]

scrump to steal fruit, esp. apples, straight from trees;
[verb]

scrupulum an Ancient Roman unit of weight –
1/24th of a Roman ounce; [Latin *tiny stone*]

scrutable able to be comprehended; [adj.];
[antonym: *inscrutable*]

sea of fog an overcast layer of fog when seen from above; a *sea of clouds* looks similar, but with wavy undulations of different lengths; [noun]; [*Wanderer above the Sea of Fog* – 19th c. German Romantic landscape painter Caspar David Friedrich, 1818]

seaborne carried by the ocean, esp. by floating; [adj.]; "*seaborne* debris"

seagirt surrounded closely by the sea; [adj.]; [poetic & rare]; [English *sea* + *girt* (to bind horizontally)]; "*seagirt* isles"

seawolf or **sea-wolf** a dangerous person or animal that attacks on or in the ocean; [noun]

seaworn or **sea-worn** noticeably worn or aged by the sea; [rare adj.]; "the *seaworn* coast"

Second Opium War an 1856-60 war in which the British and French Empires invaded China – resulted in the destruction of the *Imperial Summer Palace* in Beijing; the defeat of the Qing dynasty; and the legalization of the opium trade; [historical]

seemings outward appearances; [noun]; "And I lookt among the trees; but there did be nothing, and everywhere there did be a strange silence and a dimness of unreal *seemings*." – William Hope Hodgson, *The Night Land*, 1912

semblative resembling; suitable; [very rare adj.]

semelparous describing an animal, plant, or organism that reproduces just once in a lifetime; [adj.]; [synonym: *hapaxanthic*]; [antonym: *iteroparous*]; [Latin *semel* once]

semiglobular having a shape roughly that of a hemisphere; [adj.]; [synonym: *hemispherical*]

semipellucid only partly clear or transparent; [adj.]; "*semipellucid* glass"

semisomnia a condition of chronic low-grade fatigue caused by too little sound sleep; [rare noun]; [Latin *semi-* (half) + *somnus* (sleep)]

senex (pl. *senexes*) an elderly man; [rare noun]; [Latin *senex* elderly]

sensorial of, pertaining to, or derived from the senses or the *sensorium*; [adj.]; "*sensorial* experience"

sensory leakage when information from a normal sense like sight or hearing (rather than *psi* – a supposed psychic energy) is accidentally transferred to a person during an ESP experiment

septimation the killing or loss of 1/7th of something; [rare noun]; [*quintation* 1/5th; *decimation* 1/10th; *tricesimation* 1/30th]

sequestrum (pl. *sequestra*) a portion of dead bone or other tissue that becomes separated from the sound portion, as may happen during the process of *necrosis*; [noun]

serpentine snake-like; like the serpent in the biblical book of *Genesis*; twisty, sinuous, or curving in alternate directions; [adj.]; [synonyms: *ophidian*, *serpentinous*, *tortuous*]

seven heavens the concept of seven different levels of heaven – common to Christianity, Islam, and Judaism; in some writings each level corresponds to one of the seven *classical planets* of antiquity

shadowland a shadowy or borderline area where the normal rules of reality do not always apply; [noun]; [synonym: *twilight zone*]; "These are the *shadowlands*, places where the fantastic is not only possible, but likely, and logic & reason undergird reality but tenuously."

Shag Rocks a group of six islets 150 miles west of South Georgia, an island in the southern Atlantic; [named for the South Georgia *shag*, a seabird]

Shakespeare garden a garden with some or all of the 175 plants mentioned in Shakespeare's plays – relevant quotes are usually displayed; [noun]; "What's in a name? That which we call a *rose* by any other name would smell as sweet."
– William Shakespeare, *Romeo & Juliet*, 1597

shanks' mare a person's own legs when used for walking; "When the motorcar died from lack of petrol I hopped on the bike; soon tiring for want of air, I took to *shanks' mare*."; [noun]; [Scottish with American use]

shatterbrained or **shatterpated** wild; heedless; wandering in intellect; [rare adj.]; [synonym: *scatterbrained*]

Shavian of or pertaining to 20th c. Irish playwright George Bernard Shaw or his writings; pertaining to the Shavian alphabet – designed to ease the difficulties of conventional spelling and supported (but not developed) by Shaw; [adj.]; [*Shavius* – Latinized form of the surname *Shaw*]

Shelleyan relating to the 19th c. English Romantic poet Percy Bysshe Shelley or to his wife Mary Shelley, author of *Frankenstein*; [adj.]; [synonym: *Keatsian*]; [antonym: *Byronic*]; "Might *Mont Blanc* embody the fullest and finest expression of the *Shelleyan* sublime?"

Shire Highlands a plateau in southern Malawi – the most densely populated area of the country

Shishapangma the 14th highest peak in the world located in Tibet – it is the shortest of the world's over 8000 meter peaks, and also the last to be climbed (1964); [perhaps derived from *crest above meadows* in a Tibetan dialect]

sh*t the bed failed completely; of mechanical devices, suddenly ceasing to work with no immediate hope of repair; [rare verb]; [American slang]; "The old BMW *sh*t the bed*, so I walked back to town."

Shitterton a town in Dorset, England; "I was late returning to *Shitterton*, and had much business the following day."

shittlecock old spelling of *shuttlecock* (the racquet sport AKA *badminton*); the birdie used in same

shiver collective term for a group of sharks

shrithe to wander; to move; to creep; [rare verb]; [Dutch *schrijden* (to stride)]; "... when shadowy shapes come *shrithing* dark beneath the clouds." – James E. Miller, *England in Literature*, 1973

Siberian Traps a large region of volcanic rock formed about 252 million years BCE by volcanic eruptions spanning 2 million years; the erosion of trap rock created by successive layers of lava flow often creates a stairstep-like landscape; [Swedish *trappa* stairway]

sibilant or **sibilous** having a hissing sound; [adj.]; "Disturbing noises – tristisonous and *sibilant* – issued from the endarkening forest."

sidepiece an attractive girlfriend or boyfriend, esp. if casual and/or extramarital; [noun]; "The heiress positioned her new *sidepiece* to maximum effect."

siegecraft the warcraft of blockading a target (often

a fortress) with intent to conquer; [noun]

Silken Windhound a graceful American breed of small to mid-sized sight hounds

Silurian hypothesis a thought experiment that considers the ability of modern science to find evidence of a prior advanced civilization on Earth, perhaps a few million years ago; [named after the *Silurians* in the British TV show *Doctor Who* – a prehistoric, scientifically-advanced species of reptilian humanoids]

Silver Branch or **Silver Bough** a symbol in Irish mythology representing entry into the *Celtic Otherworld* or *Tír na nÓg*

silver cord or **sutratma** the life-giving link that some believe connects the astral body, or the higher self, to the physical body; [mentioned in the Bible book of *Ecclesiastes*]

Silverdale Hoard a collection of over 200 pieces of silver coins and jewelry found in 2011 near the village of Silverdale in NW England – dating from circa 900 CE and one of the largest Viking hoards ever found in the UK; [noun]

Silverpit crater a subsea crater off the UK's North Sea coast; [the *Silver Pit*, a nearby seafloor valley]

simianity the state of being an ape or being ape-like; [rare noun]; [adj. *simian*]

simper to smile in a silly, foolish, smug or overly eager manner; such a smile itself; [verb & noun]; "*simpering* fools"

Simurgh a winged creature like a peacock but with the head of a dog and claws of a lion – able to carry off elephants and whales; [Persian myth.]; [Sanskrit *śyenaḥ* raptor]

singular unique; peerless; extraordinary; unusual; [adj.]; "a *singular* talent"

sinistromanual left-handed; [adj.]; [antonym: *dextromanual*]; [Latin *sinister* left]; "*sinistromanual* manipulations"

Sinosphere parts of East Asia that have been heavily influenced by China or Chinese culture; China's geopolitical sphere of influence; [adj. *Sinospheric*]; "*Sinospheric* trade agreements"

sitzmark the impression left in the snow from a skier falling backwards; [noun]; [German *sitzen* (to sit)]

skeletonic like a skeleton; [adj.]; [very rare synonym: *skelic*]; "*skeletonic* old man"

skerry a small, rocky island, esp. if covered during high tides; [Scots]

Ski Cloudcroft a small American ski area near *Cloudcroft*, New Mexico

Skyriot demonym for people who live on the Greek island *Skyros*; relating to residents of *Skyros*; [noun & adj.]; "*Skyriot* generosities"

skull-collecting ant an ant species that hunts *trap jaw ants* and takes their heads back to its nest

skyborne carried by the air; in flight; [adj.]; [Old Norse *ský* cloud]

skyey resembling the sky; pertaining to the sky; [adj.] "When twilight came I ... wished some clouds would gather, for an odd timidity about the deep *skyey* voids above had crept into my soul."
– H.P. Lovecraft, *The Colour Out of Space*, 1927

slakeless not able to be satisfied; [archaic & poetic]; [synonym: *unquenchable*]; "But, I fear, the spirit of adventure – its thirst – is within me *slakeless*."
– Captain Mayne Reid, *The Rifle Rangers*, 1899

slake trough a trough of water blacksmiths use to cool a forging or a tool; [noun]

Slattenpatten a haunting female figure in Danish folklore with breasts hanging to her knees which she could flip over her shoulders when running or nursing a baby on her back; [Danish, literally: *flaccid-breasts*]

Smithian-Spathian boundary extinction a large extinction event during the early *Triassic* geologic period, about 249 million years BCE and near the boundary of the *Smithian* and *Spathian* subages

smokeshow a person that is extremely physically attractive; [noun]; [American slang]

SNAFU or **snafu** a ludicrously chaotic situation; a serious glitch or breakdown; [noun]; [from WWII military acronym derived from *Situation Normal, All Fouled Up*]

Snotra in Norse myth., a goddess associated with wisdom; [Old Norse *snotra* clever]

snoutfair or **snout-fair** having an attractive face; [very rare adj.]; [slang]

snowclad snow-covered; [poetic adj.]; "*snowclad* forests"

snowclone a cliché with the foundation of an old idiom that is altered for use in a new context; [coined in 2004 based on the supposed high number of Inuit words for snow]; "Shakespeare's 'to be or not to be' has flowered into innumerable *snowclones* of the formula 'to X or not to X'."

snowcraft the skills needed to safely travel over snowy terrain; [noun]

snowscape a landscape covered in snow; [noun]; "*snowscapes* pristine"

social battery the amount of energy a person has to expend on socializing – a social battery's maximum size varies by individual; [rare noun]; [American slang]; "He fled the party as his *social battery* neared depletion."

soigné or **soigne** (swan-yay) in fashion; elegant; stylish; immaculately groomed; [adj.]; [French]; "*soigné* socialites"

solano a hot wind that sometimes blows from the southeast in the Mediterranean, esp. on Spain's eastern coast; [noun]; [Latin *sōlānus* (pertaining to the sun, the east wind)]

solferino a bright purple-red color; the dye that produces this color; [noun]; [from *Solferino*, a town in northern Italy]

solitudinarian one who favors the solitary life; [archaic noun]

somaticize the action of converting psychological issues, esp. trauma, into physical symptoms; [verb]; [Greek *sóma* body]

somewhither to some indeterminate place; to somewhere; [archaic adverb]; [antonym: *somewhence*]; [Middle English *somwhether*]

sonder the realization that everyone else is also living a life as deep and complex as your own; [rare noun]; [a neologism coined by John Koenig *The Dictionary of Obscure Sorrows*, 2021]; [German *sonder* (without, except)]; [French *sonder* (to probe)]

sonorous or **sonoral** deep, rich, and resonant; [adj.]; [synonym: *canorous*]; "incantations *sonorous*"

soporadoratic describing one who worships sleep; one who sleeps much more than is necessary; [adj. & noun]; [Latin *sopor* (deep sleep)]; [coined by Robin Devoe in 2023]; "The *soporadoratic* youth often slept until two on weekends."

soporific something that induces sleep, esp. a drug; describing that which is very boring or sleep-inducing; [noun & adj.]; [synonyms: *soporous* & *somnific*]; "*soporific* monologues"

South Nicobar serpent eagle a bird of prey native to the Indian island of Great Nicobar – the smallest known eagle, weighing only one pound

spannew, **span-new**, or **spander-new** brand new; very new; in perfect condition; [rare]; [Old Norse *spánn* chip + *nyr* new]; [possibly originally meaning *as new as a freshly split wood chip*]

spate a flood; an overflow of water; a sudden increase; [noun]; [Dutch *spatten* (to splash)]

spatiotemporal relating to or existing in both space and time; relating to *spacetime*; [adj.]; "The manifold *spatiotemporal* considerations of traffic-flow engineers..."

spatulous or **spatulate** shaped like a spatula; [adj.]

spectatrix (rare pl. *spectatrices*) a female onlooker; [Latin]

spectral bat or **great false vampire bat** a species of bat endemic to Mexico and Central & South America – this largest bat in the New World frequently preys on birds

spectrality the quality of being ghostly; a ghost; a spectre; [noun]; "Alas, rest was not at hand for the night was frightfully punctuated with the plaintive cries of diverse specie of *spectrality*."

sphincteric or **sphincteral** of, pertaining to, or akin to a ringlike band of muscle surrounding certain bodily openings, such as the human mouth; [adj.]

spolia opima historically, the spoils a Roman general took from the vanquished leader of his adversaries, esp. when won in single combat; [Latin, literally: *the richest spoils*]

spumiferous producing foam; [very rare adj.]; [Latin *spūmifer* (foaming, foam-bearing)]; "*spumiferous* seas"

square-rigged describing a ship with roughly square sails rigged perpendicular to the keel; well dressed; [adj.]; "a *square-rigged* wedding guest"

stagecraft the skills of the theatre or of acting in staged plays; [noun]

starscape a view where stars dominate; [noun]; "the sublime *starscapes* of those boreal nights..."

starshine starlight; [poetic noun]; "...from the frosty cloudless heavens the *starshine* of a thousand constellations filtered down." – E. F. Benson, *Michael*, 1916

stellated resembling a star; star-shaped; [adj.]

stelliscript the signs in the stars that can be read to foresee the future; [very rare noun]; [coined by English Romantic poet Robert Southey in *The Doctor* (1835)]

stertorous describing that which sounds like snorting or snoring; [adj.]

stocious very intoxicated, esp. if slurring speech; [adj.]; [Irish slang]

stramineous relating to, or similar to, straw; straw-colored; insubstantial; of limited value; [adj.]; [Italian *strame* (hay, straw)]

Stregheria a neo-pagan tradition (with Italian origins) that honors a *Moon Goddess* and a *Horned God* and includes beliefs and practices similar to Wicca; [noun]; [Italian *stregoneria* (witchcraft, spell)]

strix (pl. *striges* or *strixes*) a large-headed bird of ill omen with greyish-white wings that feeds on human flesh and blood, esp. that of children; [classical myth.]; [Portuguese & Spanish *estrige* (owl, witch)]

Stymphalian birds (stim-FAY-lee-uhn) bronze-beaked, man-eating birds with poisonous dung and metallic feathers they could shoot at victims; [Greek myth.]; [the birds lived in a swamp in *Stymphalia*, a town in ancient Arcadia]

suaveolent fragrant; sweet-smelling; [rare adj.]; [Latin *suāvis* (sweet, pleasant)]; "*suaveolent* zephyrs"

suavity the quality of being agreeable to the mind; a pleasing manner; pleasantness; [noun]; [synonym: *urbanity*]; [Latin *suāvitās* sweetness]; "Such are the *suavities* of the humble-minded."

sub rosa in secret; carried out in confidence; [adverb & adj.]; [Latin *under the rose*]; [in classical myth., the rose was associated with secrecy because Cupid gave *Harpocrates* (the god of silence) a rose to keep the secrets of *Venus* (the Roman goddess of love) hidden]

subadolescent somewhat younger than an adolescent; characteristic of a *subadolescent* child; a person too young to be an adolescent; [adj. & noun]; [rare]; "His humor was crude and *subadolescent*."

subception subconscious perception; [rare noun]

sublime noble and majestic; awe-inspiring due to size, beauty, etc., esp. if also simple; describing that which is not just beautiful, but grand esp. in nature or art; something *sublime*; [adj. & noun]; [noun: *sublimity*]; [Latin *sublīmis* (lofty, exalted)]; "Night is *sublime*, day is beautiful."
– Immanuel Kant, 1764

subnormothermic having a body temperature that is lower than what is considered normal; [adj.]; "He felt lethargic, like a *subnormothermic* reptile."

sufferfest a difficult endurance activity, event, or race wherein participants generally suffer, esp. from extreme fatigue; [rare noun]; [slang]; "We first relished the sublime and wild mountain trek, but once lost, our alpine frolick slowly transpeciated into an excruciating *sufferfest*."

suffuse to spread throughout something, esp. as light or liquid; [verb]; [adj. *suffusive*]; [synonym: *diffuse*]; [Italian *soffóndere* (to suffuse)]; "The *suffusive* light of golden hour."

summertide summertime; the summer season; [literary noun]; [Swedish *sommartid* summertime]

sunblink a brief glimpse or sudden issuance of sunshine; [noun]; [Scotland]

sunbreak a phenomenon in which sunbeams penetrate a hole in expansive cloud cover; [noun]

suncapped having the top of a hill, mountain, etc. lit by the sun; [poetic adj.]; "*suncapped* pines"

sunder to break, esp. with force; to separate; to disunite in almost any manner; [verb]; [adj. *sunderable*]; "We *sunder* the walls, and lay open the inner city." – Virgil, *The Aeneid*, circa 25 BCE

sunglade a forest glade suffused with sunlight; sun reflecting on a body of water; [noun]; [poetic & rare]; "...sometimes, also, the rising or setting sun produces a *sunglade*, like a river of molten gold, or rather of pure fire, flowing across the ocean toward the earth..." – Jane Goodwin Austin, *Moonfolk: A True Account of the Home of the Fairy Tales*, 1874

sunlit uplands a place or time of peaceful prosperity; [synonym: *halcyon days*]; "If we can stand up to him all Europe may be free, and the life of the world may move forward into broad, *sunlit uplands*;" – Winston Churchill, *House of Commons Official Report*, 1940

sun-shot or **sunshot** interpenetrated, or shot through, with sunlight; [rare adj.]; "Temple stood in the stand, listening to the birds among the *sunshot* leaves, listening, looking about." – William Faulkner, *Sanctuary*, 1931

sunshower or **sun shower** a rain shower when it is also sunny; [noun]; [synonym: *monkey's wedding*]

sunswept decribing somewhere that receives much sunlight; [rare adj.]; "She promptly fled to *sunswept* climes."

superficies (pl. *superficies*) the surface; the exterior part of something; the surface of something immaterial, esp. the soul or mind; [noun]; [Latin *super-* (above, upon) + *faciēs* (shape, face)]; "An immense metropolis, like London, is calculated to make men selfish and uninteresting. ... They present but the cold *superficies* of character – its rich and genial qualities have no time to be warmed into a flow." – Washington Irving, *The Sketch Book of Geoffrey Crayon*, 1819

supraclavicular fossa an indentation just above the collarbone (clavicle) on the human body; [noun]

surfeit the collective term for a group of skunks

surprisal the act of surprising; the state of being taken unawares; [noun]

sward a patch of land covered in grass; turf; [noun] [synonym: *greensward*]

Sweet dew incident a failed coup against the eunuchs by an emperor in 835 CE during the Chinese Tang dynasty; the eunuchs gained foreknowledge of the plot and solidified power through a counter-coup; [the authenticity of *sweet dew* on a pomegranate tree as a sign of divine favor figures prominently in tales of the incident]; [historical]

swordcraft knowledge of swords or swordplay; skill in the use of swords; [noun]

symphonious of or relating to sounds that are harmonious together; [adj.]; [Ancient Greek *sún* (with, together)]

synchromism an art movement founded in 1912 by two American artists – based on the idea that colors can be harmoniously orchestrated in paintings in a manner analagous to musical composition; [*synchromists* sometimes called their art works *synchromies*]

T

Tabula Rogeriana a 70-map atlas commissioned by the Norman King Roger II and completed in 1154 by Arab geographer Muhammad al-Idrisi; [Latin

The Book of Roger; also known by a title literally translated from Arabic as: *The Excursion of One Who is Eager to Penetrate the Distant Horizons*]

tacenda (pl. only) things not to be spoken of or made public; things best left unsaid; [very rare noun]; [Latin *tacenda* (that which should be kept silent)]

tactical chunder an instance of purposefully vomiting so as to drink more alcohol or to feel better; [rare noun]; [UK slang]

take French leave to leave without saying goodbye to anyone, esp. from parties; [verb]; [synonym: *abscond*]

tardiloquent talking slowly; [very rare adj.]; [noun: *tardiloquence*]; [Latin *tardus* slow + *loquor* talk]

tarn a small alpine lake or pond, esp. if formed by glaciers and often without tributaries; [noun]; [Swedish *tjärn* (small forest lake)]

Tarnhelm, **the** a magic helmet in Wagner's *Der Ring des Nibelungen* that lends its wearer powers of invisibility and transformation; [German *tarnen* (to disguise, to hide)]

Tasman Fracture, **the** a 2.5 mile deep ocean trench southwest of *Tasmania*, Australia

tatterdemalion tattered; one dressed in ragged clothing; [adj. & noun]; "Rags mounted guard over the treasure. Virtue rendered these *tatterdemalions* resplendent."
– Victor Hugo, *Les Misérables*, 1887

teaser bitch a female dog in heat that provides stimulus for a male dog to produce sperm that is later used for breeding purposes; [noun]

technopeasant one who doesn't understand technology and is thereby disadvantaged within modern society; [noun]; [antonym: *digerati*]

temporicide the act of killing, or wasting, time;
[noun]; [archaic & very rare]; [Latin *temporis* time]

tentacular tentacle-like; pertaining to or similar to
a tentacle; [adj.]; "His embrace had a *tentacular*
quality that she found quite unnerving."

teramorphous shaped or formed very abnormally
or like a monster; [very rare adj.]; [Greek *téras*
monster]; "An unsettling variety of *teramorphous*
creatures skulked around the firelit glade's
umbratic edges."

Terra Australis a hyphothetical continent that
appeared on maps between the 15th and 18th
centuries – not based on any direct observations,
but rather on the theory that it made sense for
continental landmass in the Northern
Hemisphere to be balanced by land in the
Southern Hemisphere; [synonyms: *Terra Australis
Ignota* & *the Antipodes*]; [Latin *Southern Land*]

testaceous having a shell, as oysters; colored
dull orange-brown, like some bricks; [adj.];
"Neptunian Albion's high *testaceous* food,
And flavour'd Chian wines with incense fum'd"
– John Dyer, *The Ruins of Rome. A Poem*, 1740

tetrabard a unit of vocabulary equal to
60,000 words; [rare noun]; [neologism];
[Latin *tetra-* (four) + English *bard* (Shakespeare)];
[coined by Steven Pinker by comparing the
average American high school graduate's
vocabulary of 60,000 words to the 15,000
different words in Shakespeare's plays];
"Her vocabulary of three *tetrabards* was
quite impressive."

Theatrum Orbis Terrarum 1570 CE atlas printed in Antwerp, Belgium – considered the first modern atlas; [Latin *Theatre of the Orb of the World*]

therianthropy the process or ability to morph between human and animal form; [rare noun]; [adj. *therianthropic*]; [Greek *thirío* (wild beast)]

theriocephalic having the head of some type of animal and the body of a human; [rare adj.]; [noun: *theriocephaly*]; [Greek *kefáli* head]; "*Theriocephalic* creatures are common in many of the world's mythologies."

theriomorphic having the form of a wild animal or a beast; [adj.]; [Ancient Greek *thēríon* (wild beast) + *morphế* (shape)]; "*theriomorphic* statuary"

thermoception the perception of heat & cold; the ability of many organisms (incl. humans) to sense temperature; [rare noun]; [adj. *thermoceptive*]; [synonym: *thermoreception*]

therocephalians a group of extinct, probably carnivorous, pre-mammalian animals with relatively large heads; [noun]; [Ancient Greek *thēríon* (wild beast) + *kephalế* (head)]

Thesmophoria a widely-celebrated Ancient Greek autumnal festival with secret rituals – only open to women; [Ancient Greek *thesmós* law + *phorós* bearing]

Thetis one of the fifty *Nereids* – daughters of the ancient sea god Nereus; [Greek myth.]; [Greek *théto* (to place, to position)]

Thing of all Geats, the a legislature convened in the Swedish city of Skara from pre-historic times until the Middle Ages – all men from certain parts of what is now SW Sweden capable of wielding a weapon had the right to participate; [noun]; [Swedish *Alla götars ting*]; [historical]

Thingmen a military unit serving the Danish kings that ruled England from 1013-1051 CE – largely composed of Swedish mercenaries; [historical]

third rail a political situation, proposal, or program that would be dangerous or political suicide to get involved in or make changes to; [noun]; [from the deadly *third rail* on some train tracks that supplies electricity to a train]; "Most senators considered the subsidy program a *third rail* – even proposing slight changes could imperil one's re-election."

Thistlegorm a British cargo steamship sunk in the Red Sea by German aircraft in 1941 – now a popular dive site; [English *thistle* (national flower of Scotland) + Gaelic *gorm* (blue)]

thixotropic (thick-suh-trō-pic) describing a gel that liquifies when shaken; [adj.]; [antonym: *rheopectic*]; [Ancient Greek *thíxsis* (touch) + *tropikós* (pertaining to a change)]

thoughtworld or **thought-world** the world seen through the lenses of the attitudes, belief systems, basic assumptions, etc. of a given society; [rare]; [synonym: *zeitgeist*]; [German *Gedankenwelt* thoughtworld]

thralldom or **thrall** a state of enslavement or subjugation to a thing, person, or organization; [noun]; [Middle English *thralles* slaves]; "In those days the United States had not yet fully thrown off a certain *thralldom* of awe before European opinion."
– John T. Morse, *Abraham Lincoln*, 1899

Thrymheim the residence of *Thiazi,* a type of giant, in Jotunheim, the home of the giants; [Norse myth.]; [Old Norse *thunder home*]

Thuban, **Dragon's Tail**, or **Alpha Draconis** a binary star system in the constellation Draco; was the north pole star from the 4th to the 2nd millennium BCE; [Arabic *thu ʿbān* (large snake)]; [astronomy]

Thule the semi-legendary island noted as the most northerly inhabited location in ancient Roman and Greek cartography; [rare adj. *Thulean*]

Thulian pink a bright pastel pink shade; [rare noun]; [*Thule* – a northern, semi-legendary island of classical antiquity]

thunderblast the sound of thunder, esp. when nearby; [noun]; [synonym: *thunderpeal*]

thunderbolt a lightning flash accompanied by the sound of thunder; a particularly terrible or unexpected event, esp. if both; [noun]; [synonym: *thunderstroke*]

thunderous or **thundrous** extremely loud; describing something that sounds like thunder; [adj.]; [rare synonym: *thundersome*]

tibio-tarsal articulation the joint on a bird connecting the *tarsus* and the *tibia* – the avian equivalent to the human knee

titian a bright auburn color with a golden tint; describing something of that color; [noun & adj.]; [from Italian painter *Titian* who often used this color, esp. when painting women's hair]

titillating or **titillative** sensually activating, arousing, or stimulating; [adj.]; [Italian *titillo* (I tickle lightly)]; "Hers was a touch almost too *titillative*..."

titubant stumbling, esp. if (or as if) tipsy; [adj.]; [Spanish *titubear* (to stutter, to hesitate)]

topolatry the worship or adulation of a certain place; [noun]

toque (tewk) a brimless hat, esp. a tall, white one such as worn by some chefs; in Canada, a knitted woolen hat, often with a pom-pom atop; [noun]

tornadic like a tornado; characterized by strong winds; violently destructive; [adj.]; [Spanish *tronada* thunderstorm]; "*tornadic* outbursts"

torpescent becoming torpid, lethargic, or numb; [adj.]; [noun: *torpescence*]; "wallowing through the torrid, the *torpescent* afternoon..."

torrentine torrential; characterized by torrents; flowing heavily or in large quantities; [rare adj.]; "tempests *torrentine*"

torrid of weather, very hot and dry; full of strong, ardent emotions, esp. arising from sexual love; [adj.]; [Latin *torrida* (dry, parched)]; "*torrid* liaisons"

tour d'horizon a wide-ranging tour; figuratively, a broad survey or general summary; [noun]; [French]; [Italian *giro d'orizzonte*]

translucidus a translucent cloud – may appear in *altocumulus* and *stratus* clouds, *et alia*; [noun]; [antonym: *opacus*]

transneptunian object an asteroid or dwarf planet that orbits the Sun at a greater average distance than Neptune; [noun]; [astronomy]

transpeciate to change from one species into another; to transform; [verb]; [archaic & rare]

treacly too sweet; expressing emotions such as sorrow in an insincere or cloying manner; [adj.]; [from *treacle* – another word for molasses];

"His manner seemed quite pleasant, but soon enough he trended a bit too *treacly*."

trenchant keen; biting; forcefully clear and effective; [adj.]; [French *trancher* (to slice)]; "As heavy as an axe, and as *trenchant*, his glance fell upon me."

trichotillomania a strong compulsion or urge to pull out one's own hair; [noun]; [adj. *trichotillomanic*]; [Ancient Greek *thríx* (hair) + *tíllō* (pluck) + *manía* (madness)]

tristisonous having a sorrowful sound; [obsolete adj.]; [Latin *trīstimōnia* sadness]

triquetral having three corners; [adj.]; [synonym: *triquetrous*]; [Latin *triquetrus* triangular]

trollied being extremely intoxicated from alcohol; [rare adj.]; [slang]

trouserless not wearing trousers; "He appeared at the door shirtless... and *trouserless*; which left her speechless! and later, sleepless..."

trousseau (pl. *trousseaux*) the clothes, linens, etc. collected by a new bride, esp. if traditionally gifted; [noun]; [French]

tsuris (sir-riss) problems; hassle; [noun]; [Hebrew *tsará* (trouble, tragedy)]

tulgey thick and dark, esp. if also frightening and in reference to a forest; [rare adj.]
"The Jabberwock, with eyes of flame,
Came whiffling through the *tulgey* wood"
– Lewis Carroll, *Jabberwocky*, 1871

tumescent swollen; bloated; *figuratively,* inflated or bombastic; [adj.]; "*tumescent* writings"

tumulate to swell; to bury a corpse; [verb]; [Italian *tumulo* (mound, tomb)]; "They buried, they interred; they *tumulated* & entombed the body..."

tumulus (pl. *tumuli*) a mound of earth, esp. when placed over an ancient tomb; [noun]; [Latin]; "forgotten *tumuli* peopled the glade"

turgescent becoming swollen; [adj.]; [synonym: *tumid* or *turgid*]; [French & Romanian *turgescent*]; "The remains – pale, pink, veined, *turgescent* – were a ghastly vision."

twilitten, **twilit**, or **twilighted** lit or aglow from twilight or as if from twilight; [adj.]; [Old English *twi-* (two, double)]

Twins with the Golden Star, the a Romanian fairy tale involving the birth (and successive recarnations) of twin boys with golden stars on their foreheads

twitterpated smitten or lovestruck; [adj.]; [noun: *twitterpation*]; [first widespread usage was in the 1942 Disney movie *Bambi*]

U

uberly very much; extremely; [adverb]; [informal & rare]; [German *über-* (above-)]

ubiquity the state of being everywhere at once; [noun]; [adj. *ubiquitous*]; [synonym: *omnipresence*]; [Latin *ubīque* everywhere]; "a government both intrusive and *ubiquitous*"

Ugandan affairs or **Ugandan discussions** sexual affairs, esp. if scandalous; [noun]; [UK]; [coined based on a 1973 party incident wherein an Irish journalist, explaining why she was in the arms of a former Ugandan cabinet minister, claimed they were *upstairs discussing Uganda*]

ultima furthest; final; a word's last syllable; [adj. &
     noun]; [Latin *ultimus* last]; "Either you say
     Hesperia alone, and it will mean Italy, or you
     add *ultima*, and it will mean Spain."
     – Leonardo da Vinci, 16th c. Italian polymath
ultroneous spontaneous; voluntary; [adj.];
     [archaic & rare]; [noun: *ultroneity*];
     [Latin *ultro* (beyond, afar, of one's own accord)]
umbraculum in botany, an umbrella-like
     appendage; an umbrella; [noun]; [second
     definition very rare]; [adj. *umbraculiform*];
     [Latin *umbrāculum* (shade, umbrella, bower)];
     [Italian *ombrellino* (small umbrella, parasol)]
umbratilous shadowy; faint; vague; [very rare adj.];
     [Portuguese & Spanish *sombra* shade]
umbrose shady; [obsolete adj.]; [Latin *umbra*
     (shadow, shade, ghost)]
Umland the outskirts or hinterlands of a city or
     other settlement that are connected to the
     core through economic and cultural activity;
     [rare noun]; [German *um* (round about) +
     Land (land)]
Umman Manda a poorly understood ancient people
     whose home lay somewhere between Central
     Anatolia and NE Babylonia; [Akkadian language,
     literally: *the hoard from who knows where*]
unblooded untried in combat; having never killed
     an enemy; [adj.]; "Waves of *unblooded* youth
     were sent into the fray – few returned."
uncompanioned alone; without friends; unequalled
     in greatness; [adj.]; "His *uncompanioned* alpine
     wanderings inspired his finest verse."

undawning describing that which does not dawn; not yet dawning; [poetic adj.]; "The Present is *the* thing, for the Future does nothing (yet) and the Past is forever *undawning*."

underbred of inferior breeding or socialization; (of animals) not purebred; [adj.]; "Himself, he felt the most *underbred* of all; he was afraid of these Utopians." – H. G. Wells, *Men Like Gods*, 1923

undergrove a grove of shrubs or short trees under taller ones; [noun]; "The shrine was hidden in an obscure *undergrove* near the edge of the estate."

undernote in music, a low or softer note that acts as a background; [noun]; [synonym: *undertone*]

underthings undergarments; [noun]; "She put on the soft, beautiful *underthings* with unexpected pleasure in their dantiness." – Marjorie Cooke, *Cinderella Jane*, 1917

underweening undervaluation; extremely modest; [noun & adj.]; [rare]; [antonym: *overweening*]; "His *underweening* manner was all the more surprising, and charming, considering the power of his station."

undulate to cause to move in a wavelike fashion; to move like a wave; wavy in appearance; describing a human voice, animal vocalization, or other sound that changes in pitch and/or volume; [verb & adj.]; [Italian, Spanish, and Portuguese *onda* wave]; "The cadence of her voice then seemed to *undulate*, almost as if in sympathy to the beach and the ocean's broken wave."

unfellowed without friend or fellow; peerless; unmatched; [adj.]; [synonym: *uncompanioned*]

unfledged not yet having feathers; not having attained full growth; young or inexperienced; [adj.]; [synonyms: *implumous*, *callow*]; [Middle English *flygge* (able to fly, feathered, active)]

unfrequented rarely visited; [adj.]; "Thoughts of the *unfrequented*, sunlit uplands of yesteryear raised a swollen, nostalgic wave within him; and a single, soon-dried tear crystallized his endarkening visage as he sailed the evening breeze – toward what distant land he knew not."

ungirt unbelted; loosely belted; ungirdled; lacking in discipline; [German *Gurt* (strap, belt)]; "The youth was wild, profligate, and *ungirt*."

unguligrade having hooves; an animal that walks on hooves; [adj. & noun]; [Sicilian *ugni* fingernails]; "Are there any *unguligrade* carnivores?"

unhorsed removed from a horse's back; removed or unseated from a position, esp. if appointed or elected; [verb]; "Numerous scandals soon *unhorsed* the young senator."

unihemispheric slow-wave sleep sleep during which one side of the brain rests while the other side remains alert – used by many bird species, esp. while circling in flight; [noun]

uniquity the state of being unique or one of kind; [noun]; [antonym: *ubiquity*]

unparagoned the very best; without equal; unmatched; [archaic adj.]; [Italian *paragone* comparison]

unplumbed with depths that have not been measured; not measured in any way; [adj.]; "O the manifold dark and *unplumbed* recesses of the American mind!"

unquiet restless; uneasy; [synonym: *discomposed*];
"Thy light alone like mist o'er mountains driven,
Or music by the night-wind sent
Through strings of some still instrument,
Or moonlight on a midnight stream,
Gives grace and truth to life's *unquiet* dream."
– Percy Shelley, *Hymn to Intellectual Beauty*, 1816

unrevenued without revenue or income; [adj.];
"He was a gentleman... and dashing; and yet
unrevenued and therefore, ineligible."

unseemly inappropriate; unsuited to the occasion;
not in good taste; [adj.]; [noun: *unseemliness*];
[Middle English *semly* or *semelich* (beautiful,
appropriate)]; "His attire at court was impeccable;
unfortunately, he was rather *unseemly* in manner
as well as in speech and soon barred from any
royal audience."

unsummered without summer; without qualities or
emotions associated with summer, such as light,
warmth, or happiness; [adj.]; [poetic & rare];
[synonym: *summerless*]; "The *unsummered* city
shivers." – Louis Brodsky, *Reuben's: Early June
Morning*, 1965

untoward unfavorable; unruly; improper; [adj.];
[synonym: *immodest*]; "*untoward* behaviors"

unus mundus the idea that everything is derived
from a primordial unified reality – this concept
underlies Western philosophy and theology;
[Latin *one world*]

up the wooden hills to bedfordshire up the stairs
to bed; [rare phrase]; [UK slang]

Urania the muse of astronomy; [Greek myth.]

uranic pertaining to the heavens; celestial; containing uranium; [Greek *ránia* heavenly]; "...on I know not what telluric or *uranic* principles..." – T. Carlyle, *History of Frederick the Great*, 1865

uranomania a delusion that one is heaven-born or of divine origin; an obsession with heaven or divinity; [very rare noun]; [Greek *ouranós* (sky, roof, heaven)]

uropoetic producing or inducing the production of urine; [adj.]; "He quaffs the *uropoetic* draughts."

urstromtal (pl. *urstromtäler*) a wide glacial valley; [rare noun]; [German *ur-* (primeval) + *Strom* (stream) + *Tal* (valley)]

utopian ideal; perfect; seemingly ideal, but not practical; [adj.]; [obsolete synonym: *utopical*]; [*Utopia* – a 1506 book by Sir Thomas More describing an island with a seemingly perfect society]; "Unto his *utopian* feverdream he lay in thrall."

utopiate a type of drug that helps one escape from reality's problems and may instill dreams of an ideal life; [very rare noun]; [coined by Dr. Richard Blum in 1964]

utopographer someone who writes fictional works depicting utopias; [rare noun]; "...such latter-day *utopographers* as Skinner and Aldous Huxley..." – W. Warren Wagar, *Dreams of Reason...*, 1998

uzzard the letter z; [archaic & rare]; [synonyms: *zed* & *izzard*]

V

vacivity spatial emptiness; vacancy; [very rare noun]; [Latin *vacīvitās* (emptiness, lack)]

vacuity emotional emptiness; physical emptiness; vacuum; idleness; [noun]; "Beyond that was only the velvety darkness – the absolute *vacuity* of space that carries no sound, refracts no light." – R. F. Starzl, *In the Orbit of Saturn*, 1931

vagina dentata a toothed vagina – part of myths from around the world; [Latin *dentata* toothed]

vale of tears in Christianity, the world as a place of sorrow & difficulty; any place of sorrow or suffering; "But though life's valley be a *vale of tears*, A brighter scene beyond that vale appears, Whose glory with a light that never fades, Shoots between scattered rocks & opening shades" – William Cowper, 18th c. Anglican hymnwriter

Valhalla the place where half the slain warriors live until Ragnorak, when they will fight for Odin; [Norse myth.]; [Old Norse *Valhǫll* (hall of the slain)]

Vanaprastha the *way of the forest* – the third stage of life; the others being: *bachelor student*; *married householder*; and the fourth: *renunciation ascetic*; during *Vanaprastha*, spiritual liberation is pursued; [Hinduism]

vaquero a cowboy; a cattle herder; [noun]; [Spanish *vaca* cow]

Varangian Guard an elite group composed mostly of Norsemen whose main duty was guarding the Byzantine emperors from the 10th-14th c. CE; [historical]

Vasingtonia the Latinized name for America's state of Washington; [very rare noun]

vastity vastness; the quality of being very large and expansive; [noun]; [Latin *vāsta* (empty, desolate, immense)]

Vastu shastra a traditional Indian system of architecture, based on ancient texts, that emphasizes principles of design, layout, spatial geometry, space arrangement, *et alia* – aims to integrate architecture with nature; [Sanskrit, literally: *the science of architecture*]

vaticinal relating to prophecies; [adj.]; [Spanish & Portuguese *vaticinar* (to predict)]; "He has left *vaticinal* rhymes, in which he predicted the union of England with Scotland..." – Thomas Warton, *History of English Poetry*, 1781

veil of Isis a metaphor in which the veiled goddess *Isis* represents the difficulty or impossibility of mortals understanding nature's secrets; [based on a now lost Egyptian statue of *Isis* with the inscription: *I am all that has been and is and shall be; and no mortal has ever lifted my veil*]

veliferous carrying or bearing sails; [archaic]; [Latin *vēlifer* sail-bearing]; "The bay was dotted with all manner of *veliferous* craft."

vellicate to lightly touch a person's body so as to excite surface nerves; to tickle; to criticize in a mildly irritating manner; [verb]; [adj. *vellicative*]

vellichor (vellie-kohre) the thought-provoking nostalgia and sense of time's passage evoked by used bookstores; the smell of old books; a nostalgic feeling, melancholic desire, or strange yearning evoked by a used book

store or by the scent of old books; [rare noun];
[coined by poet & lexicographer John Koenig];
"... inhaling the paper's *vellichor*, the opium-like
scent of yesteryear and childhood."
– Sam Millar, *The Bespoke Hitman*, 2018

vendange tardive a style of dessert wine made
using a process known as *passerillage* – leaving
the grapes on the vine until they start to
dehydrate; [French *late harvest*]

Venetic an extinct Indo-European language within
the Italic subgroup spoken in ancient times by
the *Veneti* people of what is now NE Italy and
part of Slovenia

Venusian an inhabitant of Venus; of or relating
to the planet Venus or its inhabitants; [noun &
adj.]; [synonym: *Cytherean*]; "*Venusian* deities"

venustaphobia the fear of beautiful human females;
[very rare noun]; [rare synonym: *caligynephobia*];
[*Venus*, the Roman goddess of beauty]

verbing to use a noun as if it were a verb;
"No one ever said *adulting* was easy."

verboten forbidden; prohibited; [adj.]; [German]

vernal pond or **ephemeral pool** a seasonal pool
of water usually devoid of fish which provides
important habitat for certain insect and
amphibian species that fish would otherwise
predate upon

vesuviate to forcefully burst like a volcano;
to erupt with heat; [very rare verb];
[*Vesuvius*, an active Italian volcano that
erupted in 79 CE & buried Pompeii]; "He was
warned she might *vesuviate* if challenged."

viameter, **viatometer**, or **hodometer** an odometer; an instrument that measures the distance a vehicle has travelled; [dated]; [Greek *odós* road]

videndum (pl. *videnda*) something meant to be seen; [rare noun]; [Latin]; "Bored, he yet dutifully imbibed the *videnda* of his not so Grand Tour and shortly returned home to the estate he so loved."

Villarceau circles in geometry, a pair of circles produced by slicing a *torus* through its center at a certain angle; [Yvon *Villarceau*, 19th c. French mathematician]

vineries vineyards; plantations of grapes used for making wine; [noun]

vinomadefied soaked with wine; [very rare adj.]; [Latin *madida* (wet, soaked, drunk)]

violescent becoming or tending toward a violet color; [adj.]

visage the human face; the countenance or look of a person or animal; [noun];
"I met a traveller from an antique land,
Who said – 'Two vast and trunkless legs of stone
Stand in the desert.... Near them, on the sand,
Half sunk a shattered *visage* lies, whose frown,
And wrinkled lip, and sneer of cold command,
Tell that its sculptor well those passions read..."
– Percy Bysshe Shelley, *Ozymandias*, 1818

Vitosha 7500-foot mountain massif near Sofia, Bulgaria that is home to the oldest nature park in the Balkans; [known in ancient times by its Latin names *Scomius* or *Scombrus*]

vitriform looking like glass; having a glass-like form; [adj.]; [synonym: *hyaline*]; [Latin *vitrum* glass]

vivarium (pl. *vivaria*) an artificially arranged place, often an enclosure, used for keeping living animals; [noun]; [Latin]; "The expansive *vivarium* contained seven species of salamander and four of newt."

vividity the quality of being *vivid*; something bright, intense, and/or colorful; [noun]; [synonym: *vividness*]; "Butterflies – the fluttering *vividities* of that green-meadowed spring."

voiceless without a voice; mute; not having a vote; [adj.]; "...and where are thou,
My country? On thy *voiceless* shore
The heroic lay is tuneless now –
The heroic bosom beats no more!
And must thy lyre, so long divine,
Degenerate into hands like mine?"
– Lord Byron, *The Isles of Greece*, 1819

volant flying or able to fly; moving quickly or buoyantly as though flying or floating; nimble; [adj.]; [rare synonym: *volitant*]

voluminous large; having great volume; having written many books; [adj.]; [synonym: *copious*]; "She met artists prolific, and authors *voluminous*."

vulgarian a debased or distasteful person, esp. if unaware they are so; uncouth, obscene, and/or distastful; [noun & adj.]; "At meal times his choice was simple: suffer the *vulgarians* or starve."

vulpine fox-like; cunning; relating to a fox; [adj.]; [Italian *volpe* (fox, vixen)]

W

wanderoo common name for the *lion-tailed macaque*, an Old World monkey endemic to SW

India – a striking grey or silver mane frames their faces; [Sinhalese *wandurō* monkeys]; [German *Bartaffe* (beard ape)]

Wandervogel a popular movement that began in 1896 wherein German youth groups protested industrialization by hiking in the woods and communing with nature – outlawed by the Nazis in 1933; [German *wandering bird*]

War of Devolution a war from 1667-68 during which France occupied two provinces of the Holy Roman Empire, then under the sovereignty of the King of Spain; [using an obscure law, French King Louis XIV claimed the territories had *devolved* to him through his marriage to Maria Theresa of Spain]; [historical]

War of Jenkin's Ear 1739-48 war between Britain and the Spanish Empire fought mostly in the Caribbean over trading opportunities, incl. the slave trade; [Robert *Jenkins*, a British captain whose *ear* was severed by Spanish coast guards while searching his ship for contraband]

warp and woof or **warp and weft** the threads in woven fabric – the warp is threads running lengthwise and the woof, crosswise; figuratively, the foundational structure of any process or system; "The *warp and weft* of our lives..."

Watlington Hoard a collection of Viking silver, buried circa 878 after *Alfred the Great* defeated the *Great Heathen Army* – the hoard was discovered in 2015 in the English town of *Watlington*

wetwork work that involves directly killing people, esp. with guns or knives; [rare noun]; [slang]

Whipsnade Zoo a 600-acre zoo and safari park that has train service and is located in *Whipsnade*, a small village in Bedfordshire, England

whirlygigs a term for testicles; [archaic & rare]; [17th to 19th c. British slang]

whiskerando a human, usually male, with prominent or otherwise notable whiskers; [rare noun]

Whiskey Dick Mountain a small mountain in central Washington, an American state

Whiskey Rebellion or **Whiskey Insurrection** a violent 1791-94 tax protest; distilled spirits, most notably whiskey, were the first category of domestically produced product taxed by the newly formed American government; [historical]

whiskey tango foxtrot a euphemism for *what the f*ck*; [interjection]; [NATO phonetic alphabet]

wildering bewildering; perplexing; [poetic adj.]; [synonym: *puzzlesome*];
"Alas! how weak is reason's *wildering* chain!
How low we fall, from heights we seek to gain!
The lamp of Science, through the mists afar,
Fades like the sun upon the Georgian star;"
– Lydia Sigourney, *The Georgian Planet*, 1827

Wilhelm scream a stock sound effect of a man screaming, usually when shot or falling from a height, used in dozens of films, incl. *Star Wars* and *Indiana Jones*; [first used by the character Private *Wilhelm* in a 1953 western]

wine-dark similar to the dark color of some wine – used esp. to describe the sea; [literary adj.];
"Long enough the *wine-dark* wave our weary bark did carry."
– Alfred, Lord Tennyson, *The Lotos Eaters*, 1833

winelore knowledge of wine, wine grapes, or wine-making; [noun]; [synonyms: *enology* & *vinology*]

winklepicker or **winkle-picker** someone who harvests periwinkles (a type of snail); a style of pointy-toed footwear popular in the 1950s and 60s; [noun]

wintertide wintertime; [noun]; [archaic & poetic]

Witch Head Nebula a faint reflection nebula vaguely shaped like the profile of a witch's head and illuminated by the star Rigel, prominent in the constellation of Orion

Wodehousian or **Wodehousean** pertaining to or in the style of 20th c. English author P.G. Wodehouse, esp. his books detailing the adventures of the feather-brained *Bertie Wooster* and his wise and talented valet *Jeeves*; [rare adj.]; "*Wodehousian* imbroglios"

Wonderboom, **the** a 1000-year-old grove of *Ficus salicifolia* in NE South Africa, under whose shade many *Voortrekkers* rested; [Afrikaans *wonder tree*]

wondershine a beautiful, glorious, or seemingly miraculous glow or shine; [rare noun]; [synonym: *wonderglow*]

wonderworld a world or any place full of wonders and/or delights; [noun]; [synonym: *wonderland*]; [Swedish *undra* (to wonder)]

woodlore or **woodcraft** the totality of skills useful when living or recreating in a forested area

woolly rhinoceros a species of rhino with long, thick hair that lived in northern Eurasia before going extinct about 10,000 BCE – a massive hump would nourish the beast during lean times on the cold, harsh *mammoth steppe*

Wreckhouse Winds up to 200kph winds that blow across *Wreckhouse*, Newfoundland – an area of mostly flat, barren ground between the Long Range Mountains and the Atlantic Ocean

wunderkind or **Wunderkind** (pl. *wunderkinder*) a very talented or gifted person, esp. one who achieves success at a young age; [synonyms: *phenom* & *child prodigy*]; [German *Wunder* wonder + *Kind* child]

X

Xaverian a member of the *Xaverian Brothers*, a religious order promoting Catholic education founded in 1839 in Bruges, Belgium; pertaining to this group; [noun & adj.]; [16th c. Spanish Catholic missionary Saint Francis *Xavier*]

xenobombulate to avoid work by pretending to be sick; [obsolete verb]; [synonym: *malinger*]

xenodochial kind to strangers; [rare adj.]; [Ancient Greek *xenodokhḗ* (strangers' banquet)]

xerophile an organism that thrives in dry conditions; [adj. *xerophilic*]; [Ancient Greek *xērós* dry]

xylorimba a percussion musical instrument similar to a xylophone, but with a wider octave range like a marimba

Y

yard sale or **yardsale** in alpine skiing, the collection of gear (skis, poles, goggles, etc.) sometimes strewn across the slope after a dramatic fall; such a fall itself; [rare noun]; [American slang]; "Zude, impressive *yard sale*! Are you OK?"

yardang a streamlined rock protuberance carved by wind and blown sand which lies parallel to the prevailing winds, often with an unusual shape – present in most of the world's deserts; [noun]; [Turkish *yar* cliff]

yeti a humanoid animal said to live in the Himalayan mountains; [synonym: *abominable snowman*]; [derived from Tibetan for *rock bear*]

yoga nidra or **yogic sleep** a particular state of consciousness between being awake and being asleep – usually induced through meditation

yonks a very long time; ages; [synonym: *donkey's years*]; [UK slang]; [possibly abbreviated from **y**ears, m**on**ths, and wee**ks**]

young Turk a young person active in a cause that advocates for political (or other) reform; any young person with a rebellious attitude or lifesytle; [from *Young Turks*, a late 19th and early 20th century political movement for reform of the Ottoman Empire]

Z

zealotic like a zealot; [adj.]; [synonym: *fanatical*]

zenzic pertaining to the square of a number; [adj.];

zephyr a light breeze, esp. if from the west; to blow like a gentle wind; [noun & verb]; [adj. *zephyrean*, *zephyrous*, and *zephyred*]; [Latin *zephyrus* (west wind)]; "scented *zephyrs*"

zhuzh or **zhoosh** to tweak something to improve it; to spruce up; to make more appealing, exciting, or interesting; [rare verb]; [often used with *up*]; [UK slang]

ziggurat a temple tower in the shape of a terraced pyramid or compound with several receding levels; [ancient Mesopotamia]; any building with a style similar to a historical ziggurat; [noun]; [adj. *zigguratic*]; [Assyrian *ziqqurratum* height]

Zirkelstein, the a treed, cone-shaped hill with a 40-meter-high sandstone summit block in Saxony, Germany; [German *Zirkel* compass + *Stein* rock]

zonda wind a dry wind that blows down the eastern slopes of the Andes in Argentina — may exceed 150 mph; [rare noun]; [Spanish *viento zonda* (zonda wind)]

THE END

About the Author

Robin Devoe is the *nom de plume* of Rob E. Earl — an Alaskan who enjoys word-collecting, poetry, skiing, cycling, and motorcycling.

Other works (multiple editions) include: *Dictionary of the Strange, Curious, and Lovely* (2017, 2022); *Epic English Words* (2022); and *Pale Western Star: The Poetry of Robin Devoe* (2019, 2022).

Made in the USA
Middletown, DE
27 August 2024

59805249R00113